SPEAK YOUR
TRUTH

D1336218

SPEAK YOUR
TRUTH

CONNECTING WITH YOUR INNER TRUTH
AND LEARNING TO FIND YOUR VOICE

Fearne Cotton

First published in Great Britain in 2021 by Orion Spring
This edition published in Great Britain in 2021 by Orion Spring
an imprint of The Orion Publishing Group Ltd
Carmelite House, 50 Victoria Embankment
London EC4Y 0DZ

An Hachette UK Company

1 3 5 7 9 10 8 6 4 2

ISBN (Mass Market Paperback) 978 1 4091 8318 1
ISBN (eBook) 978 1 4091 8319 8

Typeset by Goldust Design
Printed and bound in Great Britain by
Clays Ltd, Elcograf S.p.A.

www.orionbooks.co.uk

For Rex, Honey, Arthur and Lola.
Keep speaking your truth forever.

CONTENTS

Introduction

HOW GETTING QUIET MADE ME LOUDER

It's not often we think about the insides of our bodies, let alone see them in high-definition quality on a screen. I more often worry about the state of my split ends than what is going on a centimetre below my scalp in my ever-whirring brain. I spend more time thinking about getting the right bra for my postnatal boobs than about the beating heart cleverly working away directly below my B cup. Yet here I am, in a brightly lit hospital room, with a small camera down my nasal canal pointing directly at the back of my throat.

Two fleshy, quivering doors are the focal point on the screen: my first ever sighting of my very own vocal cords. The two small bands of muscle in my larynx that give me my voice. I've had them for thirty-nine years but this is my first peek. The doctor asks me for a high 'Eeeeeee' note, so I breathe in and then let out a husky, breathy sound which would give Marilyn Monroe a run for her money. My vocal cords are working hard to keep the escaping air contained yet something is obstructing them, hindering them from doing their job. And there it is on the screen – a cyst! A tough little nugget positioned on the left-hand cord, stubbornly keeping the pair of them from shutting and giving me as much husk as Rod Stewart after a big night out.

Over Christmas 2019, my voice had slowly deteriorated. At first I thought it sounded sultry and sophisticated, but by Boxing Day it had become grating and slightly uncomfortable. After five weeks of wondering when my throat would clear so I could get back to recording my 'Happy Place' podcast, I knew I had to take action.

Back in the hospital room, the doctor pointed out my new little friend as I stared at the screen with curiosity. Apparently cysts are common in people who do a lot of voice work, yet as they're mostly benign they're not studied enough to accurately know how and why they develop in the first place. An operation was mentioned after which, to my shock, I would be prescribed two weeks' voice rest post operation.

On hearing this news, I felt a strange mixture of complete panic and total relief. I'm not sure which extreme forced its way to the front first. The panic certainly derived from the knowledge that I, Fearne Cotton, am a control freak. How on earth was I going to control every corner of my life without a commanding voice? My mouth moving is usually the catalyst to all action. Often I speak before the thoughts have formed as I have such an insatiable need for action. I reject stagnation, push away idleness, laugh in the face of rest. I'm not saying this is the right way to go about things but, after thirty-nine years, I know that this is my natural inclination.

My voice leads the way, it's the lieutenant motivating the troops with cadence and volume. My body and brain catch up with the shape of the words once they're out. Without my voice I would have to free fall, trust others and LET GO. That sounded like total vulnerability to me and, to put it mildly, I'm not very good at that.

And yet. Relief reared its head at the same moment, because being in control all of the time is exhausting. Even though it often feels like a coping mechanism to herd the various wild elements of my life, being a control freak requires a lot of energy. Maybe it would be interesting to let that go and let others take the reins? Maybe I would learn something, have clarity, more ideas or simply rejuvenate and gather new energy? Maybe I would learn to love letting go and allow more flow and less force into my world?

Still. TWO WEEKS of silence. I'm not sure I've managed more than two *minutes* of silence in my whole life. Although, on reflection, voice rest sounded slightly glamorous in an Adele-post-tour kind of way. Or perhaps I would be like Ariel, the Little Mermaid, with her voice wickedly stolen from her as she wobbled on freshly gifted legs towards her Prince Charming. Either way, I could see the plus side.

Two weeks though: it would be an eternity. Talking is what I do. It's one of the only things I do. In that moment, I realised how defined I am by my voice.

I often walk into shops completely unrecognised but as soon as I open my mouth to ask where the Jiffy bags are, heads turn. My voice has become familiar to people after years of infiltrating homes, workplaces and cars while on the radio. It's more recently become a companion to others on long commutes or blustery morning jogs through my podcast series. At home, my voice is my tool to supposedly keep control of chaotic family life with screeches of 'Put your shoes on!' and 'Don't balance on the arm of the sofa!'

Knowing I can say my bit makes me feel safe. How would I feel without it? I didn't feel necessarily alarmed or upset at the diagnosis, just curious. Could I really manage two full weeks of silence? How would I feel without being able to express myself? And how the hell did this cyst get there?

During the cab journey home, with a runny nose thanks to the camera that had just worked its way down my nasal canal and a numb throat from the anaesthetic, I started to really get thinking about what could have caused this sizeable cyst to set up camp at the back of my throat. I'm a big believer in unprocessed thoughts and traumas manifesting physically. I've noticed this in my own life so many times over the years. I've experienced high fevers after not processing rage properly, severe back ache during moments where I am carrying too much because I haven't asked for help and feeling nauseous when I know I'm sick to my stomach of certain scenarios that keep playing out. I didn't think this cyst could just be a coincidence.

Our throat canal is the channel to all of our expression. It is where thoughts turn to words and are either spoken or swallowed in fear, upset or paranoia. It's a salient and sacred part of our physical body that allows us to tell the world who we are and what we stand for.

So obviously I got my phone out and started googling. Not always the best idea after visiting a hospital but I was careful not to go on any dodgy websites and stuck to my usual alternative and slightly less fearmongering sources of information. Thanks to ten years' yoga practice I know a little about the body's chakras, or energy centres, and I've read way too many books on spirituality, yet I felt the need to know more about this specific area of my body.

One holistic website really grabbed my attention with its theories around the throat. According to the Hindu tradition of Tantra, the throat chakra, situated at the base of the throat, is white in colour with sixteen purple petals unfurling from its centre. It is the part of the body that is associated with self-expression and creativity. Excessive stress, namely fear of speaking out, affects this chakra greatly and can block its energy. Is this what had perhaps happened to me?

I take great pleasure in speaking. I've used my voice to put questions to some of the world's greatest minds, interesting people and leaders. I've conversed with Stephen Fry on mental health, posed questions on feminism to US Secretary of State Hillary Rodham Clinton, I've discussed motherhood with Jada Pinkett Smith. I've travelled to parts of the world where language barriers get in the way but still managed to piece together short moments of verbal exchange to forge beautiful connections in African slums and with saint-like charity workers helping with the malaria crisis. I've soothed my children by whispering gentle stories in their ear as they struggle to sleep, I've shouted loudly to break the cacophony of noise when my kids are fighting with each other. I've used my voice to gingerly ask for a phone number on a sweltering Ibiza evening, enveloped in dance music and swimming in vodka, which led to marriage and two children and two stepchildren. I've sung loudly in the car with the windows down when life felt sweet and bouncy. I've screamed and shouted when the tension of life needed an escape from my body. I've told many people I love them. I've told people I'll help. But have I always been honest? Have I always spoken my truth?

It's not something I'd thought much about before now. I know there have been moments where I have swallowed words because I've been scared. I have pushed fiery, hot, acerbic sentences down as I was scared of what might come next. I have said 'yes' when really I meant a definite 'no way'. I have dialled down my own truth because I was scared of being ridiculed. I'm sure it'll be the same for you too. To varying degrees, we have all suppressed our truth out of fear.

I wonder if I feel this more acutely than others because I've had my every word dissected, celebrated, made fun of and taken out of context since I first became a television presenter aged fifteen. Every syllable that pops out of my mouth on a broadcast has to be right. Every fact checked, each opinion considered enough not to cause concern, every joke or quip light and airy and inoffensive. The pressure can be immense. Even the very slight nervous stutter that I hadn't even known I had was ridiculed, making me so self-conscious that it subsequently plagued me for months. Every tweet and Instagram post has to be inclusive of everyone and factually correct. Every sentence transcribed into interview format carefully pondered and presented. At times, this pressure to get everything right has felt suffocating.

Spoken words never look the same written down – they lose all nuance and something said as a joke can be taken in deadly earnest – so I've had extreme paranoia in most press interviews. Anecdotes spoken aloud to journalists that weren't necessarily dramatic to live through read off a page like an Indiana Jones script, the tone and temperament totally lost. There have also been times during my radio broadcasting career where I have felt so on edge that I might say the wrong thing or accidentally offend someone that I've halved my personality just to be 'safe'. I've shrunk it, squashed it and diluted its potency to fit what I deemed would be appropriate. Sometimes I wonder if I have forgotten what I was like before I started silencing myself. Before I constantly asked myself: what am I allowed to say? What do people want to hear? What will keep the beast of paranoia and shame away? This cyst was now making me realise that the pressure to conform, and the years of worry about how I used my voice, were actually very damaging.

What if the cyst was a tangible ball of tension and anxiety, alerting me to the need for a long-overdue change? How bad could it really be if I spoke my truth?

In the dictionary 'truth' is defined as 'that which is true or in accordance with fact or reality' but I'm not sure it's that simple when we apply the meaning to our lives.

For starters, the word 'fact' slightly riles me. Let me explain. Yes, we know there are facts out there, scientifically proven notions and realities we can all agree on. The sky is blue to the human eye, cats meow, sleep is good for us – yet some so-called facts are subjective and learned. Often we give descriptions of ourselves and others using definitive words like 'I am' and 'I can never' and 'he/she is'. We'll say, 'I'm terrible with money' without questioning where this supposed fact came from, or how we might have come to believe it. I'm guilty of exactly this just a few paragraphs earlier when I confidently stated, 'I am a control freak.' But am I? Is this learned behaviour? Is being a control freak really my truth?

The truth I'm dissecting and discussing in this book lies beneath the labels we give ourselves. It sits under the opinions we profess and the things we think we know. Truth to me is so much more than words spoken, it's a feeling, an inner knowing that exudes calm and connection. You might not instantly understand that feeling and might feel unsure about what it even is, but you will have experienced it many times in your life. It can be registered as a gut feeling when decision-making is required, but it is much bigger than that. Your truth is omnipresent and constant, yet unfortunately it is often buried beneath layers of lived experience, trauma, repeated bad habits and complicated relationship dynamics: but it is ALWAYS there.

Some tap in to their truth by reaching towards the holy. Religion may secure an instant connection to all that IS. Others have worked in a disciplined way to cultivate daily practices that remind them of the truth; meditation being one of the more traditional ways to reveal what is real. Some will have had epiphanies, big game-changing moments in life where perspective is shifted and eyes are opened to the truth.

Once we understand what truth feels like we can then start speaking it. If we are always rooted to the truth, the words we speak will always be right for us in that moment. A warning: speaking the truth does not always make for a peaceful life! If you are feeling the truth and speaking it aloud you will 100 per cent piss people off, as others will have to face their own truth and may feel the need to react to yours. Yet if you keep the truth in sight then you'll be able to swim through these torrents with ease, knowing you're doing the right thing. Speaking your truth is not about people-pleasing or ducking under challenges, it's about facing up to all life experience and approaching it in a way which feels rooted to that feeling of truth.

Being unapologetically truthful all the time may sound unrealistic or maybe even ridiculous – believe me, it often strikes me this way, which is partly why I wanted to explore the subject in a book. Yet I want to feel that truth every day so I can keep growing and learning. I don't want to be road-blocked by fear or worry into being less than I know I can be. I want to waste less time in mental battles with myself, and therefore with others. I want my happiness to be based inside and not on outside influences like other people or things. I know that concentrating on the truth and what is real will be a key component to me discovering this alchemy. It will be the same for you too.

So, in that moment, on a grey Tuesday morning in the back of a black cab, I decided things had to be different. I might not change everything overnight, but from now on I would endeavour to speak my truth. At first, in small, gentle ways but hopefully eventually in big, bold brushstrokes. Part of me worried I had forgotten what my actual truth is, but don't fret, we'll get to that later. For now, I was ready for baby steps.

PING! An email from a friend, who I don't see much but like a lot, asking me to her birthday party. Here was a chance for a baby step! An opportunity to strike with honesty and MY TRUTH! I apprehensively typed:

> Dear lovely pal. Thank you so much for thinking of me! I cannot believe you're going to be forty, you look eighteen. Please start ageing so I don't end up looking like your nan. I won't be able to make your party because I've been going to bed so terribly early lately. My kids are up a lot in the night and my work schedule is bulging so I'm trying to be more practical about staying well and sleep seems to be the answer at the moment. Slightly dull but I'm sure I'll get my mojo back once the kids are a little older. Maybe I can take you for tea soon? Have the best night and a stiff gin for me. Happy birthday, darling.
> Love Fearne X

The truth, my truth. How bad could it be? Would she be offended or think of me as a desperately sad pyjama-wearing hermit? Maybe, but maybe not. And also, who cares anyway? I am just being my true and honest self.

This particular experiment went well and said friend sent back a beautifully empathetic response with a few excellent sleep tips. Weighted blankets were purchased, a white-noise machine I had in the cupboard dusted off and I wasn't socially cast aside or forgotten due to my honesty. Phew, but how long could I keep this up?

The next day of my honesty experiment brought an encounter with a slightly sexist cab driver. It was a classic case of someone saying something that he never intended to cause offence, yet still he crossed the line and pissed off this staunch feminist. Usually I would laugh politely and quickly pull out headphones to listen to Fleetwood Mac for the rest of the journey but today was different. I told him in a reasonable and friendly tone that I didn't like being labelled a 'fairy type', as he was (sweetly) insisting I was, because, as dreamy as that may sound to him, I also run a multi-faceted business which requires hard work, hours of emails, meetings, big decisions and very little fairy dust. He laughed, we moved on. My truth was spoken, I didn't swallow down and suppress the anger that could rear up later when someone barged past me in the supermarket.

If you look back at your own behaviour can you notice moments where you may have acted out later because you didn't speak your truth at the time? An obvious one that I'm sure many couples will have experienced is a form of torture I've put my husband through many times. For example, perhaps he'll ask if I mind if he goes and practises his guitar for the morning, which is fair enough considering we are both freelance creative types who have little structure forced upon us when it comes to work. We rely heavily on working through a balanced system in the home to carve out creative time individually to work and achieve what is desired. I'll sometimes say yes but feel instant anger in my chest. This anger serves to remind me that I'm not as nice to myself as Jesse is. He knows he wants to go and practise his guitar and totally deserves to. I often don't believe I deserve the same consideration of my own needs. I'm very hard on myself, so often don't give myself enough time in the day to do stuff I really want to. I'll act like a prize martyr, showing how I'm capable of putting everyone before me while really pining for some space.

The classic martyr rarely contains their frustration so the inevitable happens. Jesse wanders off to strum through Reef hits for a couple of hours after I've smiled and given him the nod, while I'm deep-breathing through rage, playing Barbie-goes-on-a-caravan-holiday with Honey. That evening, the kids will be in bed and we'll be cooking and chatting and I'll spot a small chink of weakness and proceed to prise open my cavern of rage. Jesse could be pouring the wrong amount of milk in my tea or perhaps has left the fridge open and all the anger I've stored up and obsessed over comes at him like a cyclone. Not cool on my part at all. Unbelievably not cool because Jesse is always more than fair when I ask if it's possible to go and write for a few hours or take time out for a walk in the park. He's a much nicer person than I am, FACT.

But you get my point, right? Sometimes the anger, upset or injustice of a moment will come out at a completely different point in the day because, let's face it, it HAS to come out. Emotion cannot be contained forever. It cannot dissipate unless dealt with or worked through. You can exercise it out by boxing perhaps or running fast; you could cry all night into a pillow to release upset, but the quickest and most rewarding way to move on from big emotions is to speak the truth, and usually to the other person in the dynamic.

The rest of my week of truth followed suit. Every time I spoke up about how I really felt, there was initial fear at how the words might escape from my lips but then relief. For all my worries, there was little drama and there was even a sensation of relaxation. Little tension, just free-flowing words and a sense that it was OK to be me and express myself in the way that felt best.

Now, I know this sounds rather too good to be true and I admit that I was only flexing small honesty muscles at this point. I hadn't yet had to face a huge mortifying stand-off or confrontation. But that was coming, believe me. And I think that starting small gave me a chance to experiment with my truth in ways that felt safe and built my confidence. I got a little bolder every time I spoke up for myself and that got me ready for the bigger stuff.

These baby steps were leading towards addressing the more challenging problems I've faced in life when I haven't spoken my truth, or even known what my truth is. In this book, I will look back at tougher times, mistakes made and previously swallowed words and ask myself, could I have done things differently? Would it have made a difference? I'll pose some questions and work through my own insecurities and mental blocks all in the name of experimenting and encouraging you to do the same. Is speaking our truth as awful as we imagine? Will being true to ourselves feel terrifying, excruciating or really rather freeing?

1

TRUTH IN ISOLATION: COVID-19

This past spring of solitude has rocked our world. As I write, we are distanced from others, trapped behind doors, stripped of everything that we consider to be part of normal life and with a lot of time to look at ourselves. None of us could have imagined such a time and such a seismic shift in thought and energy, almost overnight. We weren't prepared. We have assumed that in our privileged lifetimes, in our safe country, we are free to work, shop, love, fight, travel, plan and complain without any concern at all. But we are IN IT. At the time of writing this book, the Covid-19 pandemic is blazing through society at a terrifying speed with no one sure as to what will happen next.

We are battling through fake news with clean, dry hands grappling at the last loo roll. We are working out our own personal limits of how much news we can digest without imploding from fear. We're distanced yet desperately trying to stay connected via HouseParty, Zoom, FaceTime and Instagram.

In some ways, in this unprecedented time, the essential truth of humanity has been forced to the surface. The truth has always been that, as humans, we seek connection and are a kind and altruistic species, but these traits often get masked by the wants of the modern world. We forget about our elderly neighbours because we're late for the school run. We don't check in with our cousin who lives alone as we are bogged down with late-night work emails. This pandemic has pushed our truth from the bottom of the pile of modern-world rubble and has shone a light on what really matters.

It's also demonstrated to us the truth of how to live life – by living in the NOW. As a huge fan of Eckhart Tolle, and his bestselling book *The Power of Now*, I'm no stranger to this theory and yet over and over again I ignore such wisdom. I think what lies ahead is better and at the same time I am haunted by the past. I plan ahead and try to control things, even though ultimately I know there is no way to control the future.

As I write this, schools are closed, supermarket shelves are bare and the health service is overwhelmed. We can only live minute by minute. We have no clue as to what the future holds. We have no idea of the final death toll, the financial loss, the emotional fallout, the strain on relationships. We cannot look ahead as no one has the answers. Looking too far ahead would also only spike fear. We must be in the moment and deal with the daily washing of hands, scrubbing of clothes, cooking every leftover, planning our shopping trips thoroughly and facetiming family.

We can only deal in the day-to-day. Yet this is how we should always live – in the present moment. For me, this is the biggest truth of them all and yet we trample all over it in favour of imagining the future might be better. Perhaps unusually, I have learned that I feel much less anxiety living in the now, even under these lockdown conditions.

At first, I felt I had so little control over what was happening that I became obsessive about cleaning the house. Each day, I tackled a new room, junk cupboard or drawer, bleach in hand, attacking chaos where I could. I'm now gradually starting to let go and it feels pretty good. Bloody hairy at times as I'm a Virgoan control freak with a penchant for order, but I'm loving just appreciating the olive tree in the garden – and the fact that I'm fortunate enough to even have a garden – the coffee I prepare each morning, the blue sky we've been so lucky to have above our heads and other delicious minutiae. I feel better in that truth. Perhaps you did too?

As well as the world's global truths rising to the surface like urgent bubbles in a boiling pan, we've had to navigate our own truths staring us in the face, whether we like it or not. This situation has removed all the distractions and now it's just us, at home, with nowhere to hide! My truths have become urgent and obvious and unavoidable.

I can tell you about them now. It might even help me to do so, as I'm still figuring it all out. I have demons and I have truths and I often run away from both, burying myself in work and daily chores. I will distract myself with planning podcasts and brainstorming Happy Place initiatives, I will think up new books to write and festival ideas, I will buy birthday presents five months in advance, rearrange furniture in bedrooms, paint old cupboards . . . anything to run away from the truth. I like to tell myself it's not avoidance because it's productive, but this time at home has made me face the truth: I am running from myself with busyness.

These last two weeks I have had to SIT WITH IT! Sitting with your truth, as we have discussed, is not always easy. I am working a little from home on this book but mainly I am home-schooling my kids and slowing the hell down. I haven't slowed down in years. It is scary. This slower pace has offered me the gift of less anxiety but it has also made me aware of how much my self-worth derives from success and my career. I realise that my supposed success, and others telling me that my work is good, helps to keep the under-lying self-loathing at bay. Which leads to a ridiculous and nonsensical conclusion that I am only worthwhile, and worthy, if I am successful. That sort of thinking won't survive in this heat!

I have been forced to look at several truths. First up, the truth that I need to find self-worth in just BEING and not doing. I must find my self-worth in those moments where I am in dirty jogging bottoms praying my kids will attempt some schoolwork after breakfast. I have to find it in the moments where there is no time to do work emails because I'm code-cracking maths sums with Rex. I have to seek it in the moments I'm appreciating the magnolia flowers and bright blue sky. I'm sitting with it, I'm working at it.

The truth is, of course, that I have worth with or without whatever we define as success. The truth is we ALL do. Our worth is there in our sparkling eyes and calloused palms. There is worth in our smile over the fence to a neighbour and in the total solitude we experience while reading books. It's there in our beating hearts and puffing lungs. We don't need to have or to achieve anything to feel worthy. We don't need a partner, a fancy job, posh clothes, the ability to speak another language, the skill to cook a poached egg. Our worth is simply THERE already.

I know I'm not alone in these feelings. Many of us will have found this enforced stillness has challenged our ideas about worth and success, and many of us will have battled with this. New thoughts and new ideas offer up discomfort. These troubled times are all about discomfort in so many ways, but we all have to remember that is where the growth is. Getting past being uncomfortable is how we will change, morph, mould and expand to allow our truth to manifest in every way possible.

How we communicate with others is imperative too. If we are in a house with a partner, parent, kids, or all of the aforementioned, we have to be able to say our bit. For my family and most likely for yours, it's unusual for everyone to be in the house all the time. We normally have school, work, chores, errands or exercise to give us breaks from company. Not while Covid-19 reigns. We are cooped up without a clue how to cope with the relentlessness of constant connection. Subject matters that you've previously been able to get around or ignore with a partner may now be inescapable. You might need to ask for space and quiet. You could realise there are even more things that irk you about this person than you had imagined.

I feel very lucky that in these times Jesse and I get on well. We balance each other out. I am full throttle into the home-schooling with printed-out sheets, boxes of arts and crafts and a stringent timetable that I clock regularly. Jesse is laid back so is offering up words of wisdom but also allowing time to just be. He is taking care of sport and activity in the garden, creating obstacle courses and silly games I haven't the physical energy for. I love him being home as he normally tours with his band so much which can create resentment on my part as I feel I'm doing all the childcare alone. When he is home there is an equilibrium that allows our best sides to shine. Well, most of the time. Of course, there have been disagreements, sleepless nights and angry whispers out of earshot of the kids, but for the most part we are good.

The kids seem to love being home and having us around twenty-four-seven – it makes us happy to see them content and relaxed in this new strangeness. Jesse and I have been very honest with each other when we need time out. I went for a solo walk in a secluded, unpopulated area today as I had a low-level headache from all of the worry I have about friends who are not coping as well. I'm devastated for those who have already lost family members, in bits for those struggling to keep small businesses afloat, in knots for single parents who have no one to share the load and in complete gratitude for those on the front line of the NHS. I have no words to express that last one. Thank you simply doesn't cover it. All of this is spinning round my aching head, so to have a small break from the kids arguing with each other or telling me they hate the dinner I just cooked allows a small oasis of much-needed calm.

For those who live alone, this moment presents an opportunity for honesty in new ways. One of the hardest ways to be honest is to ask for help. Those who feel they are alone and stuck with no one to turn to can find themselves in a dark place. Solitude can of course be sublime, and a much-needed retreat from the chaos of life, but for those struggling it can be the worst option available. In those moments, people need to be truly brave and truly vulnerable and to reach out to someone on text, FaceTime or on a call. I know it can be hard to simply ask for a friendly voice, or regular check-ins, but you will almost certainly be met with understanding. The hardest part is asking.

I'm certainly trying to check in with everyone I know who is having a tough time in solitude. On Jesse's side of the family, there has been a lot of pain, so it has been imperative we stay focused on connecting regularly with those we know need a little love. Small gestures are HUGE in these unprecedented times so we are making sure we check in daily with those who need us.

The first two weeks of lockdown brought sadness to Jesse's side of the family with an unexpected loss. A relative who always had a bright smile, oodles of talent and an unforgettable mischievous laugh. It was a total shock. White noise ringing in our ears. A quickened heartbeat as our minds tried desperately to process the news. At this point, this pandemic got very REAL for us. The truth that this virus isn't just happening in other parts of the globe was painfully brought home. It will affect many, whether it be through grief, pain, shock, job loss, anxiety, loneliness or lack of support.

Jesse's grieving family members were then left in isolation, dealing with acute sadness alone, which is perhaps the cruellest part of this pandemic. To not have family members by our sides and hands clasped in hands is unthinkable. So many in our country and all around the world are showing strength we didn't think was possible. The strength to give and cope alone. This strange, challenging and sad time has opened my eyes to human strength and made me pinpoint-focused on reaching out to those who need a little regular hello.

The truth is powerful at the moment. We can't ignore the fact that the planet is healing while we humans lie dormant. Canals with dolphins jumping high, green parrots in my local park, birdsong the loudest sound in the sky! Nor can we ignore that renewed sense of community that's emerged and needs to be honoured and continued. Neighbours are shopping for one another and making regular calls to those in need. There are Instagram Live workouts, singing lessons and discos connecting us all to each other. We have woken up to the fact that we must appreciate the little things in life as they're not a given. Toilet paper! Who knew we would appreciate one of life's most underestimated and boring household goods so much?

And we must remember that, like all persistent nudges towards honesty, this situation will keep showing up for all of us unless we make positive changes to honour it going forward. If we don't take note now and listen to the sound of TRUTH then we will just have to keep learning these lessons again and again.

For me, the learnings I want to take away from the lockdown are:

Stillness. I know I have to learn to enjoy, or at least accept, stillness. It's my nemesis and, in the past, stillness has had the ability to send me spiralling into a depression as I'm so fixated on thinking busy equals happy. If I don't learn this lesson during this extreme time I'm not sure I ever will. It's my number one priority.

Gratitude for the NHS. I'm feeling utterly grateful from the bottom of my beating heart for our National Health Service. I don't think I was alone in totally taking it for granted, giving the hard-working staff much less thought than they deserved. Now, like many, I have started to see the NHS less as one unit and much more as a team of brave individuals who work tirelessly to help the sick. As we've been touched personally by the virus during the Covid-19 pandemic, I cannot show my gratitude enough. Each Thursday I stand on the street and clap until my hands hurt. Each Thursday I feel bowled over by emotion, my throat constricting and my eyes prickling with tears. Why have we not done this before? We have to keep this gratitude always, for they are on the front line helping to stop this ever-growing suffering. We must all keep clapping.

Appreciating the little things. I want to hold tight to this new-found appreciation of the small joys in life. As we all do, I get so bogged down with feeling the need for the big hits of happiness. I want big success at work, big words from others, big experiences to draw from. But this period is about the small. The cloudless sky, the peaceful night sky untouched by planes, finding the right Lego piece my son desperately wanted in a box containing 7,000 tiny pieces, making a meal out of random leftovers to avoid leaving the house again. Small, small victories.

Saying I love you. I must keep telling everyone in my life that I love them and care as much as I have during this time. I have texted, facetimed, whatsapped and even called (despite how much I HATE speaking on the phone) more than I have in my whole life. I've felt the pull to tell all of those I appreciate that they're brilliant. Why has it taken a pandemic to shift my arse into gear with this one? I've even sent random postcards for fun to my best mates with stupid stickers and private jokes penned in pink ink. This I must keep up.

Looking out for my neighbours. I mean this in a very literal sense rather than religious. I have spoken more to my next-door neighbours during lockdown than I have in the six years we have lived in our home. Each day my kids scramble on garden furniture to peek over the wall at our neighbours and then revel in telling them what they've made out of cardboard boxes that day. They've swapped kid movie reviews and showed off Lego creations while I've baked homemade lemon drizzle cakes to pass over and offered to buy extra bread and cheese if needed. Our neighbour on one side is eighty-eight, so Jesse has taken extra care to ensure he is fed and well, something we shamefully hadn't done previously, assuming his family would take care of him. Of course they do, but we live centimetres away so need to up our game to make sure he knows we are there if needed.

Connecting with nature. My connection to nature has been deep during these last few weeks. I have walked to the park (while socially distancing at all times) and wandered off into parts of it that I'd not bothered to explore before. Eyes wide, drinking it all in, I've seen parrots in trees, deer lounging in the sun, squirrels dashing gleefully up trees and fat, fluffy bumble bees buzzing nearby. In these moments, I have this huge perspective shift and see the curvature of the horizon. I remember I'm a small bunch of cells roaming around on a giant floating ball and that is always rather humbling. This feeling needs to stay.

Getting creative. I've never been so inventive with cardboard boxes in my life. At first, I thought this lockdown would mean buying tons of schoolbooks and searching out online tutorials and getting every board game and toy out of crammed cupboards – but really all you need is a cardboard box. So far, out of cardboard boxes we've made: a car park for Rex's cars, two unique pirate ships complete with pirate hats and a hook arm for Captain Rex, a tree house for Honey's collection of small animals and a skateboard ramp that very quickly buckled. This sort of creativity is essential for kids and adults for time out and using our brains dynamically. Boxes can stay!

What would your lockdown learnings be?

_____

_____

_____

_____

_____

_____

_____

_____

_____

_____

_____

_____

_____

_____

_____

_____

_____

_____

_____

_____

_____

_____

2

WHEN DID WE STOP SPEAKING UP?

Each of us is born a beautiful, fuzzy peach-like ball of pure honesty. We screech with every inch of our newborn might, tiny lungs puffing like miniature bagpipes, when we are hungry, uncomfortable or tired. As babies, we care little about shattered Mum or Dad snoring nearby. Our instinct kicks in and we want milk so we shout about it. We don't care that our parents have had four minutes' sleep in the last week and we don't mind waking up other siblings in the process. We know what we want and we ask for it. Newborn babies enter the world with an inbuilt setting for honesty. At first, we speak our truth with noise and physical movement, which can be as obvious and understood as formed language – just ask a parent.

When toddlers are grappling with speech for the first time, this honesty can be practised in the most toe-curling way for their parents. I remember when my son Rex, who was around four at the time, asked a friend of mine, 'Wow, what has happened to your eyebrows?' Said friend had recently experimented with dyeing her eyebrows ahead of a party and they had gone a shade or three too dark. It was impossible to look anywhere else on her face but at the marker-pen-thick dashes above her eyes. Now, whereas I – a socially conditioned adult – had had the same thoughts as Rex, I had pushed them to one side in favour of small talk and tea, but Rex said it as it was. Every parent will have had flushed cheeks due to a small child loudly declaring that someone in the supermarket smells strange or is wearing 'weird' clothes. It's bum-clenching stuff but at this point in a young life, honesty seems the only option. Kids don't see the point in disguising their thoughts on the world, no matter what anyone else thinks.

I clearly remember being on holiday in Bournemouth back in the eighties with my parents, brother Jamie, Aunty Helena, Uncle Martin and the Cotton cousins. On the last day, we were packing up to drive back home when I had a really strong urge to go for one last dip in the pool. Swimming pools have always been the most exciting and exotic thing to us Cotton kids so I knew I couldn't say goodbye to the seaside without one more dive in the pool. But Mum said, 'NO, we haven't time.' I wailed. I begged. I pleaded. Still a no. We walked out of the reception of the hotel to have a family photo on the steps out front. Every Cotton grinned dutifully, knowing that this moment would be captured forever. Except for me. I sat with a face of thunder. I didn't give a toss. I was pissed off and I wanted everyone to know it. This particular photo still makes me laugh out loud when I see it. I can almost feel my frustration leaping out of the photo album.

I often still feel like that little person in fluorescent cycling shorts, angrily furrowing my eyebrows when things don't go my way. It's not always easy to admit as I would far rather tell you I'm super easy-going but I am not. I sprang out of the womb ready for action and needing to get shit done in my own way. I have never been one for recovering quickly from being told NO. I mope and moan and often try to blame others, so when I think back to that photo, and that sense of being denied, it's a reminder that I haven't changed that much. These days I have the emotional intelligence to find some positives in the NO and will see areas where I can learn. I know that if I'm told no today (and believe me I have been told no SO many times, in work and life) that maybe it will be an opportunity for me to try another route or open another door. I will still feel pissed off FOR SURE but I'll mope a little less and look for other options.

The other difference is that, back then, I would openly sulk and grimace when someone said no (nearly always Mum), whereas in later life I got very good at covering those feelings with fake smiles so as not to cause harm to others. And I confess I sometimes still do this. I'm smiling sweetly yet suppressing all emotions, and will either bitch about the irritating moment with a close friend or store up the anger for a later, unrelated date.

I've been conditioned throughout childhood, as most of us have, to keep those big emotions for later. We are told that passers-by are staring and judging, we are told that our behaviour is inappropriate and inconvenient, so we learn to tame it. To suppress what we are really feeling. We are trained like animals to align not just our behaviour but our emotions with what society deems appropriate. Obviously, kids have to be given the behavioural tools that will serve them well later in life, but I think most of us take the emotional suppression too far in adulthood. We feel too worried about social exclusion to speak our truth or show how we feel, so often we don't speak at all.

EXPRESSING JOY, OUR INNER CHILD AND ORANGE SUNSETS

As well as speaking up, kids are also able to let their feelings shine through in the most beautiful way. If my daughter sees a puddle on the way to school, she will dance through it in her polka dot wellies, showing the world how much joy she feels. She has no regard for the outside world's acceptance or annoyance, or worries that she might get wet or dirty, she just waltzes through the moment feeling that fleeting happiness and truthfully expressing it. When we are lucky enough to get away to overseas sunshine as a family in the summer, my kids' ritual, when hitting the beach for the first time, involves them skidding face first into the sand as they reunite with the concept of Mediterranean warmth. Pure joy emanates from their body language amid yelps of summertime euphoria. Again, they care very little what nearby sunbathers may think of their unadulterated bliss. They are happy to show their truth without restraining it, or compromising it, for the outside world. They are experts in demonstrating their truth.

At times, I can connect with my own inner child and

therefore my own simple truth. As an adult, I get there through meditating, experiencing beauty in nature and loss of thought in that moment, or by digging deep beneath the omnipresent low-level tension of being a responsible adult. If I get still and quiet enough to cut through all the brain chatter about logistics of school runs, work pressures, concerns and worries about the past and future, then there is my inner child.

In my mind, my inner child is always sat on the swing at the end of the old garden of the mock Tudor semi-detached home I grew up in. In the summer, when the air was hazy and the clouds were candyfloss, I would sit and simply swing for hours. When I say hours, I'm sure this is not a childhood, rose-tinted exaggeration, as I vividly remember Mum calling me to come in and go to bed as the last of the day's sunlight peeped shyly from behind the garden shed. I had no other distractions in these golden moments. No one to talk with, certainly no mobile phone as they were yet to be invented and no real worries. I would swing enthusiastically, kicking my legs high up towards the glimmering stars and letting gravity pull me back like a pendulum across the suburban night sky.

When I think back to this version of myself, I am mainly struck with a feeling – not thoughts or ideas, just a beautiful, bold feeling of happiness which bordered on euphoria. I didn't want to be anywhere else in the world. My euphoric joy came from simply looking at the ever-changing shades of the sunset and feeling the sun's decreasing warmth on my skin. I felt free and supported by the universe, so strongly that I can evoke those same feelings when I think back to those nights. I needed nothing more back then than my swing and the sunset, and I was perfectly happy being me. The idea of being somehow different, changing for the better or improving, would never have entered my head. I was naturally grateful without understanding the concept of gratitude and content without knowing there was any other way to be. I'm not sure I have felt that way as much in adult life.

In everyday adult life, I often assume I'm doing something wrong or could be better or should repent for my sins in the past. I have tried to emulate that sunset-gazing contentment by achieving success at work, by associating myself with interesting people or by seeking validation from outside opinions. We all know that these endeavours are never the route to ultimate contentment and understanding who we truly are but it's so hard not to fall into this trap. Back then, on the swing, I was feeling my truth. I *was* wholeheartedly my truth. Without words, I would sing my truth to the night sky and let that feeling rock me into a blissful sleep after I answered my mum's call to come back inside in the house. That blood orange sky and free-falling motion of the swing was enough for me, and I was enough for me too. I was ENOUGH. When I feel stressed, anxious and distanced from my own truth, I try to hook back in to that younger version of myself.

This morning, for example, I was feeling stretched and stressed and had started to blame others for my pain. That feeling of judgement is always an obvious sign that I am not speaking my truth on any level. As soon as I start pointing fingers, I know I have lost my way. So, instead of pushing on with work, I got into bed and put on an eye mask and did a guided meditation which unlocked the firmly closed door to what I am really about.

I sank deeply through the years and ended up back on the swing. The air was balmy and I was happy being me. My young thoughts about life were more trusting and optimistic than they are today; I was still very innocent and untouched by the outside world's scarier side. I was yet to understand the news; the internet didn't exist and I hadn't experienced any level of trauma. I just felt supported by the energy around me and was very aware of this energy at a young age. That might sound slightly out of the box for a kid but I remember always having feelings of being connected to nature and feeling alive when immersed in it. I was the stars and they were me. My skin didn't stop at my fingernails but somehow moved with the night air. This sense of connection to everything and access to my own truth has been, at times, beaten out of me by outside noise, mass opinion and verbal abuse from strangers. I'm so glad I can still connect with this memory and feeling when I need to, as it helps ground me and get back to basics.

My eye mask was soaked with tears after this meditation. Some of those tears were of sadness for the times when I've let myself forget the innocence and faith of little Fearne, but there were also tears of joy from knowing the same trust and optimism must still be in there somewhere. For me, connecting to the child I once was is the starting point in finding my truth – we'll talk more about this in a moment.

PEER PRESSURE AT SCHOOL AND THE ODD ONE OUT

If a child comes from a safe and supportive family environment, they feel they are safe to speak their truth at home. If they scream and shout and have their say, no matter how stressful it might be, their parents/parent/carer will still love them. At school, it's different. For the first time, kids have to look at how they fit into a social system and how that makes them feel. The opinions of others begin to carry a weight they didn't before and children start to question their truth.

I clearly remember trying to copy my mate Lucy's handwriting in class as she had the most formidable curvy letters as well as the neatest, shiniest hair. 'O's ballooned out in lavish bubbles and 'f's had a decadent flick that looked as if written with a quill. I think my twelve-year-old brain must have assumed that I too would feel as calm and cool as Lucy looked and could possibly reach hair-shine levels to match. Lucy and I are still great friends to this day and she still has the shiniest hair you've ever seen. I do not, but the handwriting stuck and I can still bosh out a pretty impressive curly 'f' when I need to.

We want to be accepted by our peers so much that often we dilute our own truth or take on someone else's to ensure we're part of the group. It starts in childhood but we take it with us through into our adult lives and adapting ourselves to fit in can be something we do almost unconsciously.

In secondary school, I learned a lesson in speaking my truth as I suddenly became the anomaly. I was the teenager who didn't quite fit in and who dared to be a little different.

OK, I was no Greta Thunberg, trailblazing a new way for the youth and speaking my truth to a worldwide audience, but I was doing it in my own small way. I landed my first TV job at the age of fifteen and felt like I could express a side of myself that had previously been invisible in a world of homework and freezing-cold netball matches. I had energy and excitement within me and so many words that needed to be expressed. I was bursting with ideas and big, naive dreams. I would go to Cannes with Leonardo DiCaprio, I would marry a member of Hanson and probably be best friends with the members of All Saints. I wanted something for myself other than drinking Hooch in our local park (although, of course, I did that too).

School didn't seem to be the place for those sorts of ambitious thoughts and I often felt a restless need to escape the suburbs and experience something new. I once told a teacher that the careers advice form I had filled in had been processed incorrectly as I didn't want to be a teacher but instead an actor. The system designed to take in my carefully filled-in information can't surely have led to the job description 'teacher'? As a thirty-nine-year-old today I am full of admiration for all teachers, but at fifteen years old becoming one didn't fit into my dream life. My teacher said that it was highly unlikely I would become an actor so I should give that thought up now and just knuckle down to my studies. Of course, I enthusiastically ignored that advice and went to every audition I could.

I somehow fluked my way onto ITV in 1996 with a wide grin and a pocketful of Fruit Pastilles. I loved every minute of learning about the cameras, interviewing the likes of

Cleopatra and B*Witched and eating cooked lunches from the canteen which, to my amazement, were FREE! I couldn't believe it. The whole thing felt like a dream and at last I had found an outlet for my boundless teenage energy.

Becoming a face on television inevitably made me somewhat of an oddball at a very bog-standard suburban secondary school. Names were shouted from across the lunch hall, grapes were thrown at snack break and I got used to the 'Who does she think she is?' stares. Yet I didn't care. I had full confidence in what I was doing and it didn't matter what others thought. I used to be so good at speaking my truth even when judged and ridiculed. I admire that fifteen-year-old me; today I'm much more delicate and easily knocked.

Dismissing the ridicule of my peers might seem like a small personal teenage victory – I wasn't fighting off a terrible illness or facing great adversity – but I managed to keep speaking my truth even when others tried to humiliate me. And it occurs to me, looking back, that this is something I have gotten a lot worse at over the years. Perhaps we have to work even harder as we get older to remember our truth and how little outside opinion matters?

THE MAVERICKS, PACK MENTALITY AND UNTYING KNOTS

We are all socially conditioned on some level to stay in line with what is deemed appropriate. And it's important, of course, to understand the reasons for limits and boundaries set by parents, teachers, bosses, religion and the government. At the time of writing, for example, I might feel like it's essential for me to go out and see my friends, but I understand why my family and I have to stay indoors for the safety of ourselves and others during the pandemic.

Yet many of the external rules imposed on us, and internalised by us, are something we can challenge and question. And indeed, we know that great and positive change has come as a result of incredible mavericks boldly and fearlessly questioning the status quo to create great change. The suffragettes, Martin Luther King, Malala Yousafzai, Billie Jean King, Emma Gonzalez, Greta Thunberg. They have all, alongside so many others throughout history, used their voices to say something daring and brave and new. Despite social conditioning, propaganda and indoctrination, they have had the courage and the independence of thought to form their own beliefs. Not only that, but they were able to communicate their challenging opinions to the masses in ways that have resonated and caused ripples throughout society. They will have known that speaking out would lead to controversy, uproar and personal pain, yet they still did it. They released their truth into the wild with passion and will because they knew that the consequences of silence were worse than the consequences of speaking up.

When I think of these inspirational figures, I ask myself, how did they overcome the social indoctrination and heavy outside opinions, not just of individuals, but of governments and the media? Maybe they were born with a predisposition to tell the truth? Perhaps they had wonderful mentorship from someone special? Maybe they had one teacher or adult who helped them to lift off the weight of society's expectations? In each case, they had to overcome their fear before they could speak their truth.

Historically, as humans, fear would have been founded in pack mentality. For our ancient ancestors, being part of a tribe or pack was essential for survival. Sourcing food and shelter and keeping young children alive was a group endeavour and staying firmly put in that pack was what kept you safe. Perhaps there is a part of our brain that really hasn't moved on from this pack mentality as much as we have scientifically and culturally?

Today, for many of us, concern about access to food and shelter for survival is not an everyday thought. I am of course not oblivious to the utter, heartbreaking poverty that still ravages communities and families across the world and in my own country. In this instance, in this book, I'm talking to those of us fortunate enough to have access to books and food and the time to ponder such questions.

So if conforming to the pack's expectations is no longer a matter of survival, why is human connection and acceptance still so important in adult life? This fear of being left out of the pack still seems to dominate our thoughts, so when we are teaching our children, or guiding our young through life, we instil this fear in them too. We do this by conditioning them to fit in and not make too much of a fuss. As kids, we learn to be a team player and stay in line so we stay safe. This prehistoric fear remains an undercurrent and a potent driving force for our behaviour.

As kids, we absorb these fears from our caregivers, who may be adults who have their own issues around abandonment, trauma, loss and exclusion. It's natural that we will pick up patterns of the generations before us and we cannot blame those who raised us, who are themselves acting out of their own conditioning.

I spoke at length about this with Elizabeth Gilbert when she came on the Happy Place podcast. Her brilliant novel *City of Girls* is focused around a group of women in New York City in the 1930s and how they are socially stifled and ostracised when they don't stay in line with the feminine ideals of the time. We spoke about how that weight of oppression and expectation must have affected that generation of women and our own grandmothers. It then led us to look at how, in turn, that has informed who we are as women today.

My own gorgeous nan, Sylvia Savage (I KNOW, great name!), was evacuated out of London as a child during the war and stripped of all comfort and familiarity to start a new life in Wales with a carer who treated her very badly. On her brief permitted visits back to her family, they saw that she was covered in bruises and marks on her skin. She endured terrible amounts of abuse and a deep lack of love that impacted her greatly. This experience inevitably had a knock-on effect on her ability to cope with stress later in life and how she parented my mum. This conditioning continued into my mother's own story of how she brought me up and the fears she unknowingly passed on.

Fear is passed down, from an adult to a child, who becomes an adult and passes it down to their child, and so on – each generation trying to make positive changes but also taking a little of the fear and social indoctrination with them. It's a hard cycle to break and one I look at a lot in my own parenting of my kids. None of us are perfect, that's for sure, and it requires a lot of compassion and love to look at our parents as flawed people who were doing their best with what they themselves had inherited. I now look back at that chain of inherited fear in my family with empathy and understanding. I could never imagine being subjected to that brutality as a child or being parented with that fear in the air. Take a look at your own family tree and ask yourself how fear might have been passed down the generations. Has any of this fear curbed or muted your ability or willingness to speak your truth?

Once we have a better understanding of why we may have been told as kids to keep quiet, stay in line, dilute our excitement, anger, sorrow or joy to fit in with our surroundings, we can then start to get curious and look at how we might untie those tightly woven knots.

SHUT UP, SIT DOWN, DON'T MOVE

In your childhood, did you have a teacher, parent or guardian who repeatedly told you to diffuse or water down a certain trait of your personality? Was there a teacher who told you to stop dreaming? A parent who continually told you to stop talking? A relative who said you were too loud, slow, fidgety, angry?

I'm sure most of us can remember being told to quieten down and now, as a parent, I see myself fall into this trap continually. I am not immune to embarrassment when out in public with my kids. If Honey or Rex are messing about in a restaurant, climbing on chairs and shouting that they hate the food, I will usually start to go a little red and hope no one is watching. On a good day, I'll remain calm and remind my kids that they need to behave in a way that respects the location we're in, the people who made the food and those who are bringing it to us. On a not-so-good day I may sternly insist they sit right down as all the other children in the restaurant are sitting nicely. I know that option A, where I'm not shaming my kids with an unnecessary comparison or a fear of what others think, is a much better way for them to keep all parts of their personalities intact. The language used in disciplining our kids is important – we must encourage them to flourish as their true selves as well as guiding them towards what they need to learn when they go out into the world. We need to teach them empathy, responsibility and kindness but without damaging their own truth and self-belief. Believe me when I say I know this is tough, especially when tired and triggered. It's something I'm constantly working on myself.

You can no doubt recall painful memories of your own childhood, where teachers and other adults told you NO or shamed you into regretting your behaviour. Once you've recalled these moments, you can start to think about whether they've had a lasting impact on how you act as an adult. Have you diluted your truth to please others? Were you taught this as a kid? If so, what part of you took the hit? Can you focus on that missing bit you have internally filed as 'inappropriate' or 'wrong'? Are you willing to bring it back to life and give yourself permission to feel free again? I am.

I know there are portions of my truth that have been wrecked and bruised due to social conditioning and I am eager to breathe life back into them. I've forgotten a lot of them from early childhood as I had such an extreme experience as a teenager with a LOT of outside opinion. I clearly remember being told by one TV producer during my teen years that I needed to 'pull back' a little. Meaning I needed to dilute my full-throttle approach to communicating with the audience and trust they would still like me. I had assumed before this that I needed to give my presentation to camera 110 per cent to be noticed and liked yet he was telling me to dial it down. I was able to listen, process and take on board what he said, which might have improved my on-screen persona and delivery somewhat, but I also think it left me with a huge dose of insecurity. He was essentially telling me at the time that I was 'too much'.

I think in today's society we've all been told we are 'too' something. Too skinny, too quiet, too loud, too brash, too lazy, too large, too moany, too quirky, too demanding, etc. It's a way of others controlling you to make themselves feel better, yet I believe none of us are 'too' anything. I've had to unlearn what I was told as a teen by that producer so I can align with my truth. At times, my truth is to be full-on, in your face, passionate and loud about stuff and that is A-OK.

In the moments where you feel a little lost or don't feel you have the energy to speak up it is sometimes possible to connect to your inner child. I think going back to explore that early childhood conditioning might be one of the most impactful ways for me to connect with my truth. Who was I and what did I believe about myself and others before I got tamed? Who took the wild out of me and which bits do I want to bring back to life? I can perhaps forgo the throwing spaghetti on the floor in restaurants part of my inner kid, but maybe there are parts of my younger self that, if unearthed, would serve me well in adulthood. When we've connected to who we used to be, it is time for us to find out what our truth really is.

MY INNER CHILD IS

★ Free as a bird

★ Not somebody who worries what others think

★ Inhibition-free

★ Creative

★ Playful

★ Inventive

★ Curious

★ Optimistic

★ Excitable

★ Bossy

★ Adamant

★ Determined

★ Always in cycling shorts

Now it's your turn.

My inner child is:

_____

_____

_____

_____

_____

_____

_____

_____

_____

_____

_____

_____

_____

_____

_____

_____

_____

_____

_____

_____

_____

3

WHAT IS MY TRUTH?

Everybody has a story of who they think they are. Most of these internal narratives derive from outside judgement, past experience, habit and what we are taught.

I believe myself to be a friendly person who likes cooking and painting. I am a mum who sometimes manages to stay patient and calm and at other times feels like a failure. I am someone who gets overly excited and is highly enthusiastic yet I recognise that I'm someone who also can spiral off into pitch-black darkness. I believe I'm good at my job but lose confidence easily. I sometimes feel I don't cope with life, work and everything else as well as my peers do. I love cats and hate celery. Can't drive on the motorway due to anxiety and the threat of panic attacks. Love staying in and shudder at the thought of a nightclub. Need a lot of sleep but do love an early morning.

But how many of these beliefs about myself are my truth and how many come from outside noise and what I've learned to believe? How much of my truth is a story I've just repeated so many times that it feels true? It can be tricky to let go of the stories we believe about ourselves as often they've been around for years, but what is behind those learned traits? What is beneath the story?

More recently, I've been trying to work it out for myself. Not long ago, before the pandemic, I took myself into the middle of the park where the ferns had gone brown and the sky was wide. There was little noise, just the occasional plane overhead and the screech of a bird. There were no cars as I was not near a road and no one was nearby to see me or pass judgement on the half-pyjama, half-clothing scenario I had worn for the school run. My phone was on airplane mode so I wasn't tempted to look and couldn't hear its incessant beeping. I was disconnected from the constant scroll of social media; the never-ending mind bombardment. There was no comparison to others because I couldn't view how far my mate had just run or what new job one of my peers had just celebrated on her Instagram Stories. My truth felt a little more alive. The stiller I was, the clearer it was. I felt calmer, less agitated, less concerned what others might be thinking. It might have been an ephemeral moment but it was a short glimpse at my truth that is supposedly lying dormant in there most days, I just choose to numb it with *stuff*. Social media, texts from mates, an endless supply of work emails, chores, cooking, finding odd socks, rearranging cupboards, shopping for things I don't need – ANYTHING but locking into my truth. Procrastination of the highest degree. Keeping busy so I don't look too hard at what is really going on for me.

We rarely give ourselves any time or space to find out what is really going on inside. We spend so much time online absorbing what everyone else thinks and consuming outside opinion that we start to believe it is our own. Thoughts merge and opinions stick like glue. With judgement clinging to us like Velcro, we lose our sense of self. Instead, other people's acerbic, triggering words shape our internal story about who we are.

This is a ridiculous example in many ways, but it's a simple way to show you what I mean. In dance class as a kid someone said my hair, pulled back into the traditional ballet bun, made my forehead look like a giant egg. I have never worn my hair back since. I bear no lasting grudge or deep scar but this seemingly insignificant comment affects my behaviour to this very day. Because of someone else's thoughts, I tell myself, 'I'm a person who doesn't like her forehead.' That's someone else's truth I've been carrying around for decades. What might you be carrying that doesn't belong to you?

At times, I've pushed a wheelbarrow of negative comments around with me. I've unknowingly carried around a mountain of other people's thoughts and words and become so used to them that I've believed they were my own. I got to the point where I believed these opinions were who I was. It's taken me a long time to understand: that's not my truth, it's someone else's. I'm still working on it.

This is not a sob story. I'm well aware I do a job I love and I appreciate that being in the public eye comes with often painful scrutiny, but that does not mean it hurts any less. Being known and judged by thousands of strangers isn't natural and, I believe, is too much for a brain to handle. I have been told I'm useless, annoying, a piece of shit and everything in between by people who've never met me. When I was just twenty-five, I read an article by a 'journalist' who wrote that it was unfortunate my bungee cord didn't snap when I took part in a Guinness World Record attempt at a reverse bungee. I mean, let's keep on brand with this book's message and now, all these years later, 'speak my truth' . . . What a fucking c***!

Anyway, you get the point. I've had it all chucked my way. I've also had people tell me I'm amazing and the best they've worked with but if you're going to believe the opinions of others over your own, does ANY of it matter? The negatives or positives? Allowing anyone else's story to become a part of your truth is just adding more weight to the already complex story we've built around ourselves.

There was a point, when I was in a deep depression that spanned a couple of years, where I would grab hold of any negative comment about myself and believe it to be true. Each comment fed the unruly and erratic beast that was my damaged mind. I lost all sense of what I believed to be true and who I was. I was too scared to just be me.

During those years, while engaging in weekly therapy and sometimes on medication, I left jobs and worked less. Not because I didn't love my work but because I was so scared to be in the public eye. I felt too delicate for judgement, too broken to be exposed. Sometimes I still am. I became quieter and more anxious and fearful. When I look back, I recognise that was the first warning sign: a life where you are not authentically yourself is one of fear. When you're not living your truth, when you've edited who you are to please others, or lessened parts of yourself because it feels too difficult to just be you, you feel constantly on edge, almost waiting to be found out. You know you're not being true to yourself and it leaves you fearing a judgement you may not be able to handle. It's not a relaxing way to live at all.

OPENING THE DRAWER OF SECRET STUFF

At this time of my depression, parts of the media industry I used to enjoy or had previously found unchallenging suddenly became very scary. I was convinced that failure was waiting for me everywhere. This heavy depression and anxiety forced me to look at life differently, in ways that challenged and surprised me. After some time, I began to see that when I had a panic attack at night or found myself crying in my car, these moments were signs. My truth was trying to reveal itself in a rather dramatic and difficult way and I had to listen. I knew I had to honour my truth and not resist it if I wanted to feel better.

Panic attacks are something I still deal with to this day. Another hit me between the eyes at 11 p.m. just recently as I desperately wrestled with my duvet and willed myself to sleep. As I stayed wide awake my heart raced faster and my thoughts grew uglier. I was due to take part in a TV show via Zoom as the pandemic continued to keep us on lockdown. Live TV has, for some reason, become a trigger for my panic. Years of worrying I might cock up or say the wrong thing in a live broadcast has led to an incredible heightened sensitivity to being in this space. My body is telling me in these moments, 'You are not safe.' It's screaming at me to put the brakes on. Intellectually, I know I can do the job, and have years of experience behind me to prove it, yet my body says no. This always leads to much rumination and self-inventory. Maybe my body is right. Maybe I don't need to be putting myself into stressful situations. Perhaps my priorities have changed and the ways I enjoy communicating the most are writing and podcasting, where I feel safe and connected to my audience. Maybe that's OK.

The inner battle rattles on as a part of me is disappointed that I can no longer do some of the things I used to find easy. But I can usually settle on a form of truth that feels right for now. Maybe one day I will be able to take part in high-profile live television again and feel safe but for now I respect my truth: I cannot and that is OK. Maybe this will lead me to other interesting ways of working as I have to think outside the box a little? Maybe I can once again look at why I feel the need to push myself at work so much to keep my poor drowning self-worth afloat? There are always positives and interesting things to look at in these times.

In the aftermath of a panic attack, or when feeling very low, I have always learned something about myself. I have either had to let go of something I thought I needed or consider new options and routes which I think is always a positive thing to do. The truth is sometimes that we cannot cope and sometimes we do need to make changes in life. If we resist these changes, our bodies often scream out for attention until we can't ignore our needs. I'm a little better these days at noticing when change is needed. These moments might feel tricky and painful but they are also a chance to grow and learn.

What unfurled within me from this period of depression was a much more authentic version of myself at work. I had to let go of all of the things that I had previously thought would bring me happiness and success and re-evaluate everything. I grew up in an industry that celebrated numbers and perfection. The bigger the audience, the better. The more pristinely presented the show was, the better. Slowly, over many years, perfection became my number one enemy as I felt I would always fall short of it. The more I strived to be perfect, the less brilliant I felt as I couldn't keep up with an unrealistic ambition.

The kind of work I do today only exists because I'm willing to look at flaws, mistakes and a total deconstruction of what perfect even means. Before my big career change, I knew that I felt unhappy under large amounts of pressure at work and didn't enjoy the exposure I was having to deal with on a daily basis. The need for perfection was eating me up as I felt less than perfect inside. For a long while, instead of looking at why these feelings were emerging, I covered this new truth with more work but eventually it rose to the surface. Truth came bursting out of the seams and showed itself to me.

As I began to get in touch with my truth and my more authentic self, I stepped down from many of the jobs I was best known for. I knew that certain parts of my life and working life didn't serve me anymore and were stopping me from understanding my own truth. Leaving Radio 1 was a big part of this. The daily pressure to deliver and never mess up left me feeling shattered. Speaking to the nation every day went from a beautiful privilege to feeling like a burden. I had to step down so someone else could take that platform and do it justice. Clara Amfo luckily stepped right in and is still doing the most phenomenal job on the show. Giving myself space away from the relentless churn of chasing other people's ideas of success allowed me to think what true success at work looked like for me.

I feel the first time I really honoured my truth at work was when I wrote my first book, *Happy*. Before this, my career had been all 'flashing lights, nice dresses and smiles to camera (no matter how you're feeling on the inside)'. *Happy* was about who I really was and what I really wanted to say, written in my own voice. It was the first time I had mentioned the word depression in a public space and represented my first steps in showing an audience what had really been going on for me. I lifted the glittery veil of what my life might have looked like to explain that it felt a lot different underneath.

I'm not sure I have ever felt more nervous about a work project than the night before *Happy* hit the shops. There were moments where I literally fantasised about breaking into my local Waterstones overnight to burn every copy before people could get their mitts on it. Talking about my actual, honest life as opposed to my life as Fearne the shiny TV presenter felt unnerving. Several well-meaning people had warned me that once I had talked about my depression there was NO going back. Even though fear presented itself to me in gargoyle form most days leading up to publication, I still felt it was worth the risk. What had I to lose? The old way of working was failing to deliver the feelings of connection I loved, so I needed to take a new chance.

Speaking my truth in this book opened me up to a whole new world. I met incredible people who spoke the same language as me, was presented with new opportunities that allowed me to immerse myself further into this conversation about being true to yourself and discovered new thoughts and a much better understanding of who I was. I allowed myself to be less entertaining and much more, well, ME. I wrote in a soft tone that felt natural to me, rather than the fast-paced, energetic one I had been conditioned to believe was better. I had never been encouraged to show any of the real bits of myself before. As a presenter it was impressed on me that I had to be happy, upbeat, occasionally funny, quick-witted, and fast. I couldn't allow room for people to get bored or switch over to another show. Just keep being happy and quick!

For years, I thought my truth, the real me, was too dull to show to the world. I assumed I could only illuminate the shiny bits of myself. I didn't see the worth in my truth: my darker side, my troubles, my insecurities and quirks. I kept them hidden in a drawer bulging with disorganised thoughts and concerns that I steadfastly ignored. I kept the drawer shut and kept believing that I could only honour the supposedly positive parts of me. My truth was more complex than I wanted to admit to myself and it wasn't as happy-go-lucky as most would have assumed. I was only ever talking to an audience using 50 per cent of who I was, yet when I allowed the WHOLE of me to talk and connect with others, that's when I really started enjoying myself.

PRESSING PAUSE AND LETTING GO OF WORRY

The only reason I was able to work out what my truth was and start over again is because I gave myself a short pause from the non-stop life I was living. It is of course not realistic for everyone to just stop what they're doing in life and have a break – and that's not technically what I did either as I had a young family and other ongoing work commitments. So even if we're unable to stop, we can at least find ways to slow down – and sometimes the universe finds them for us, like a coronavirus lockdown. I believe if we can find small, safe spaces to slow down and embrace simplicity, the answers will be there for us.

For me, it was about working out how to gain those moments where you can be unencumbered by noise and distraction and then learning to sit with what comes up. This needn't be something as dramatic as a year out, a sabbatical or clean break from everything. It is allowing yourself the space for thought without interruption and you can do that anywhere. Of course, there are ways in which this has been traditionally practised for centuries – meditation, yoga, a hobby that takes us out of the mind and into the body, like painting, golf, knitting, running. The action itself is just a tool to get you to the space you're looking for. That's where your truth lies. That's the place where you can just BE and understand how many of the worries you have about yourself don't matter at all.

Letting go of our worries and issues is a hard concept to embrace. We want to believe that all of our problems have meaning, otherwise why have we wasted so much time worrying about them? Of course, the big life situations do matter – health issues, our children's safety, being able to feed ourselves and have a roof over our heads, facing past traumas that stop us from living well. There are consequences if we do not tackle these parts of life with energy and care but so many of our smaller, everyday worries are forgotten within the week.

Mostly we want our enemies to stay our enemies so that we have a channel through which to vent our anger. It's easier to stick with a familiar narrative that we are useless or unworthy because then we don't have to try again. It's much harder work to start over than to stick with things as they are. However, while it might require more effort to make changes to our thought patterns, it can only benefit us in the long run. When we worry less about the small things, we regain the time wasted on negative thinking and have an opportunity to learn about ourselves rather than pointing fingers at others.

When you find that space and stillness, you may find your truth underneath all of the mental rumination, worry and outside noise. It might be buried very deep, on a subterranean level beneath stories and lies, assumptions and relationship dynamics. We know that speaking our truth can be tough, so we often stick to the destructive stories and definitions of ourselves instead. Sometimes I make excuses based on past experience so I don't have to take action and speak up. For example, I'll tell myself I'm no good at confrontation so I don't have to make the effort to say how I feel. I use the excuse of moments when I got hurt in the past to avoid forging meaningful connections with others. I allow my scrapbook of memories and mistakes to dominate my truth. I get lazy and feel I don't have the energy to be honest, yet I know deep down that my truth deserves to be honoured and that I should always pick the more interesting, unknown and scary option of truth over habit.

LOVE IS ALL YOU NEED

During the writing of this book, I discovered a new podcast called 'GABA'. In between marathon writing sessions, I would give my numb arse and achy typing fingers a break by walking in the park with headphones in. The GABA podcast gave me some much-needed space and clarity at a time when my head felt full of words. It is a wonderfully weird audio journey of storytelling, meditation and ASMR (autonomous sensory meridian response) that wakes up a part of you that might have been left behind. On my first listen I cried so hard my throat felt it was on fire (perhaps another nod to my truth needing an escape route). Afterwards, I felt very peaceful. My creativity peaked and my focus improved because, after that release, I was more connected to my truth.

At the end of each episode, Adam Martin, the podcast's creator, says, 'Love and kindness, that's what it's all about.' YES, that is it, isn't it? Love and kindness. We all know this deep down but forget most of the time. Life gets confusing, boundaries are crossed and pain is chucked our way, but really, it's just all about love. That's the truth for all of us.

You might think 'love and kindness = truth' sounds

fanciful or whimsical but it is true. It is true and it is HARD. Love can be really hard work because it requires a heavy heap of discipline. First, we must start with loving ourselves because once you've cracked that, loving other people is easy. There are times when I really, REALLY don't like myself. As I've previously mentioned, I am tough on myself so if I feel I've failed or could have done something better I mentally beat myself up. I come to a warped conclusion that I am a shitty person who doesn't deserve kindness, making it very difficult to love myself or anyone else.

If we go back to thinking about our inner child then we can remember how that self-love and true self-acceptance feels. I'm sure, like me, you were not a wandering whirl of benevolence as a kid. Of course we all made mistakes, annoyed others and did things we were told not to. Yet we didn't spend hours beating ourselves up afterwards or pummelling ourselves with self-hatred. We might have gotten a telling off, but more than likely we brushed ourselves off and carried on. If we were repeatedly told we were bad, naughty or useless as a child it is more than likely that the accumulation of those moments affect us more as adults than it did when we were kids. As adults, we see the potency in what we deem as good or bad behaviour, whereas when we are children we perhaps don't have the capacity to give it too much thought.

Remembering we are OK whether we are reaching our goals or not, the most popular person in our group or not, on top of all the house chores or not, coping with life or not, means we can connect to self-love, no matter where we are at in life. Acceptance of ourselves exactly as we are, without conditions, is not a notion we can digest once and apply instantly. This sort of self-love requires dedication. It needs to be regularly exercised to become a habit rather than forced. There are many ways we can connect to this love.

I often need complete distraction from my own tormenting thoughts. If I can muster the energy to paint or draw, I can then remember I'm good at something and that helps to elevate my mood. Practising something we know we enjoy like painting can be a good way to rise above self-loathing, but is perhaps a temporary fix. I think long-term, omnipresent self-love comes from somewhere different and I'm still on the road to discovering it. One of the ways I try to practise self-love is by daily affirmations inspired by Louise Hay and her brilliant books.

I'm a huge fan of Louise and *You Can Heal Your Life* has become a book I pick up regularly, not just in SOS moments. The book is an in-depth look at how we can free ourselves from negative habitual thought patterns to improve our lives and health. Affirmation plays a huge part in Louise's method of healing and it's something I've been trying out with lovely results. Each morning when my eyes are still glued shut and my body is limp and warm from the duvet, I use one of Louise's preferred affirmations and repeat in my mind 'I approve of myself'. I repeat this for a few minutes to remind myself I may have made mistakes, have regrets and behaved badly but I am human and that is OK. I am not flawed or 'wrong', I approve of every bit of ME. This is my route to self-love. I have to do this every day as I know my propensity to talk badly about myself but for you it may not need to be a daily practice if you're already halfway there.

When we have made peace with ourselves, or are at least on the road to believing in that self-love, then it is much easier to be kind to those around us and not just the ones we already love. Is there a person in your life where just a mention of their name irks you beyond belief? Oh my god, it is hard not to bitch and berate! So to do the absolute opposite, to send love, requires true love of yourself first and also some deeply ingrained compassion.

To feel compassion for others, we must be aware of and OWN our personal mistakes and transgressions. If we remember how fallible we are and how we have made bad choices and treated others badly then we can start to forgive and perhaps even send love in the face of utter annoyance and irritation. Again: NOT EASY. I'm not typing this from a standpoint of having mastered this one, believe me, I'm on the road to recovery with you. Today I may have taken a positive step forward but next week I may take ten back, yet I'm always willing to try to improve and to expand my own life with self-love and love for those who challenge me. This is all about creating new good habits.

Beneath the surface of our chaotic, messy, beautiful lives is love. Sometimes it may seem to be masquerading as something completely different to love, but really, we all just want love, right? If you think about something you know you're not sharing with the world – an opinion or feeling you're suppressing and keeping out of sight – you'll know you're withholding it because of fear. It is important to be able to recognise our fear because it will often illuminate something that is actually really important to us. If we are not being truthful with our partner, or don't feel we can communicate with our work colleagues honestly, or are hiding our needs, sexuality, dreams and desires, it is because we are scared of rejection – because what we really want is love. We want connection, yet sometimes the way we behave suggests otherwise.

From observing my own behaviour and from being in many friendship and family dynamics over the years, I have come to realise it is so much about wanting proper connection and ultimately love. If you know someone who finds it hard to show their emotions and is stand-offish you may assume they don't want or need love. Perhaps you even think they don't have love for you, but isn't it more likely that their behaviour is simply informed by a huge dose of insecurity?

I'm lucky that most people in my life happily show up with all emotions firing but I've been around those who don't. In the industry I've worked in, and these days tend to dance on the outskirts of, I've met MANY who seem stand-offish and very robust in their opinions. My reaction to seemingly confident people like this has been to assume that I am uncool, unworthy and that all of my weaknesses are obvious to the eye. I can think of individuals now who I deem more intelligent than me or cooler than me (which to be fair doesn't take much!) who make me feel unlovable because they seemingly don't need anything from me. They don't need my kindness and they certainly won't offer any back. Instead of noticing the insecurities that ignite their stand-offish behaviour I tend to allow my self-esteem to wither.

And yet usually these hard-shelled types are the people who need the most love. Their unwillingness to show emotion is usually a form of self-protection, their armour shining brightly in the sun, warding off anyone who might make them feel a little vulnerable. Really, like the rest of us, they just want connection and love. That's what we all want deep down. Only this morning I bumped into someone I've worked with a couple of times who is successful and confident. I shouted out 'hello' with overly enthusiastically waving hands and was met with a cold 'hi'. The chat was a little awkward and then they excused themselves without introducing me to the friend they were walking with. I was left feeling like such a plonker and wondered if perhaps I am too needy/uncool/boring/annoying and that's why they fled so soon. Yet if I take a step back and inspect the situation maybe, just maybe, this individual has insecurities and fears that keep them cool and distant. Maybe I shouldn't take it so personally at all?

Your friend who bitches constantly about the same person only does so out of their own fear of not being loved, or perhaps being unlovable. I've been that person. I've allowed my own insecurity and self-doubt to lead me into unnecessary comments about others I feel inferior to. It's as if I feel like diminishing their good bits will make my bad bits look less awful and then I'll be loved. Now, we all know that doesn't work, yet most of us have given it a bloody good try. When you feel yourself slipping into judgement of others, it is always a wake-up call about something that is going on with you.

So often we don't feel lovable and that stops us speaking our truth. We feel we don't look 'right', always say the wrong thing, come across to others as too loud or too quiet, never make good decisions etc., so we berate ourselves and tip into self-loathing. I know this has been a huge downfall for me over the years. When I take others' opinions on board as if they were my own I can often hear an explosion of abusive comments in my head about how awful I am. I'm desperately trying to change this bad habit because a bad habit is all it is. It is NOT the truth. Yes, I may have made mistakes in the past, and I'm sure you have too, but that doesn't change my truth or who I am.

Our reactions and behavioural traits are all based around our reaction to love. We are either showing love and sharing it, or scared it'll go, or feeling like we don't deserve it. If you really tune in to it now, can you feel the omnipresent hum of love that is in your heart always? It might feel trampled on due to heartache, heightened due to new love, lost altogether due to pain from your past but it is in there, always. Though it often gets exhibited very differently and is disguised as something else entirely.

For some who feel disconnected from their inner love, anger might demonstrate how much they want to feel that connection. Those who have been told they're unlovable may show how they have forgotten about their own inner love by pushing people away. Those who are scared of their own inner love and what it means to their lives may lie, hurt others or try to take another love. Most behaviour comes down to wanting to feel love from ourselves and others. We might currently think our truth is compromise, or eternal pain, or lacking, but there are layers to peel back. Sometimes we need to get the old peeler out so we can identify what is at our very core.

SITTING WITH IT AND SINGING LOUDLY

When I was younger, I'm pretty sure I thought my truth was to be successful, to be always seen and heard. God, slightly cocky, but also, why did I feel that need? What was lacking in my own self-love that nudged me to need to be so seen and recognised by others?

Possibly it was just simple teenage naivety. I felt my destiny was to experience success, to work hard to see results, to mimic others in my industry and keep getting BIGGER. Perhaps I believed that more success would bring me something I didn't already have or embody? I was young and dazzled at times by the shiny lights. Eventually, in my thirties, my showbiz expiry date ran out – it just didn't fill me up anymore. I felt empty so I had to look for new ways.

I think when we get bored or complacent in our lives, it's a good sign that we know deep down the way in which we are channelling our truth might need to be updated. So, this was the point in my life – when I found myself questioning the career I'd worked so hard for – that I gave myself a little space and time out to sit with everything I was feeling. It was scary, as, since I was young, I had filled my life with work. But sitting with the worry and fear that I might never work again was a crucial part of the process in unearthing what my truth really was in the context of my career. I'm not sure when it happened, as I think the process was very incremental, but I was gradually able to sink beneath the surface to look at the bare bones of the situation – what made me tick, what I deeply yearned for and what action I could take next.

My truth has always been that I like to make people feel good and included, yet I had only explored one way of doing so – by entertaining them and always being shiny and happy. Up until this point, I hadn't even realised there was a truth behind all of my decisions at work. I just thought I was climbing the ladder of success. Now, in stillness, I was starting to understand there was a hidden drive and truth behind my actions: connection and making people feel good.

A small sliver of time out allowed me to understand this truth and look at new ways of connecting. This discovery led me to start writing and eventually to the podcast, Happy Place Festival and more books. These days new ideas appear more rapidly and with more ease, and new people, who share the same beliefs, enter my life at the right time. Because I'm much clearer about what I want to achieve and how I want to do it there is a new breeziness to parts of the job and I enjoy my work much, much more.

If I look carefully, I can see how that clarity also applies to my life outside of work. Life always feels messier and more complicated than work to me, so in that space my truth is much more clouded and muddled. If I trace back time, I can see that my teens, twenties and thirties shared similar themes but I acted them out in very different ways. My youth consisted of strong drinks and singing out loud. The dance floor was my church where I would sway and jolt to the pulsing of a beat. Gig venues were a place of release where I could connect with others and sing in unison. Friends sleeping on couches, sinks full of bottles, friends of friends I'd only just met helping themselves to whatever was in my fridge. Some of it was fun, some less so and yet, though my life today is very different, I think my truth then was the same as it is now. I have always loved connection to others and I have enjoyed feeling part of something bigger than myself.

In my teens, I found I could connect with and create community with other like-minded people through music. It became our language. Our allegiance to a band gave us instant family. We knew how to dress, how to speak, what to drink (always a Jack and full-fat Coke). The music gave us all the answers. These days, I honour that connection-loving, community-building part of myself in different ways. My truth remains the same, yet now it looks like cooking Sunday lunches for mates and checking in with those I know are struggling. I find myself in new communities due to the work I do around mental health. New friends made, a new language needed, new topics discussed and much less Jack Daniel's and full-fat Coke – yet, running through it all, the same love of connection. It's interesting to look back and see how our truth manifests differently over the years while staying rooted in its essential nature.

PAINFUL TATTOOS AND RUNNING FROM THE TRUTH

Sometimes we travel so far from our truth that it feels out of sight. Like many people in their twenties, I experimented with every version of myself, yet rarely the truth. I wanted to run far from where I was born, far from my parents' opinions and desires and far from who I was. I felt the real me was far too boring to be valued or heard. I wanted to be interesting, quirky, cool, colourful, fun, wild. None of these tags necessarily feel natural to me and that is probably why I wanted them. These days I know I'm interesting by just being me but I'm not quirky, or 'cool', and I'm definitely not classically wild. (I say 'classically' because more recently I define 'wild' as a sense of freedom in any shape. To me, wild is often the opportunity to be small and quiet.) But back then I actively wanted to push against who I naturally was.

This manifested in a very physical way at first. I dyed my hair black with a white streak at the front, as a cool girl I was hanging out with had the same. I wore vintage clothes picked up from trendy shops and matched them with ludicrous shoes. I sat for painful hours while an artist tattooed my back, chewing lollipops to stumps to release the stress. I hung out in dark bars with low ceilings and pretentious cocktail menus. I went to gigs every night with people who looked cooler than me. I then dyed my hair bright red to be more like Shirley Manson, burying the supposedly boring mousey blonde hair with my supposedly boring personality. I caked on more eyeliner – thick black streaks to give my big round eyes more edge. I wanted the softness to go. I wanted to be cool. I wanted the real me gone. I think I assumed that if I buried my supposedly boring self I would feel more confident and like I had a place to speak and be heard. I tried to paper over my fears by emulating other people's aesthetics and actions. I actively ran from my truth and went off on an adventure of exploration.

I don't think there is anything wrong with a bit of teenage exploration – or self-exploration at any age. In fact, I think at certain points in your life that kind of experimenting is crucial for growth and learning. But looking back, I wish I had honoured a little of who I was. I didn't see that there was worth in my quiet, introverted side. I didn't see the worth in my natural looks. I didn't see the worth in just being me. Also, side note, I HATE 'cool' now! The sort of cool I was chasing back then is surface cool. The vapid and flimsy cool that looks ace on Instagram but is fucking boring in real life. Now I believe the REAL DEAL cool to be people who are simply 100 per cent themselves. Now, that's cool! Think of those who you feel are awesome; I bet you'll find they're people who aren't ashamed or scared of who they are. Luckily all of my mates fit into this category, and I love them because they are 100 per cent themselves. No editing, filtering, mutating, manipulating, emulating – they are just THEM.

A friend I've made more recently, who inspires me enormously, is Bryony Gordon. She is 110 per cent herself. She's not only herself and accepting of herself, she'll tell you about everything, right up front. Her comfort zone seems to be alerting you to her previous mistakes and supposed horrors. She wants to get all the ugly stuff out of the way first to show you how content she is with the truest version of herself.

Within minutes of meeting her a few years ago, I knew the trauma of her drug-fuelled wedding night, her struggle being newly sober and her bra size. WHAT MORE COULD YOU WANT? It's not even a test to see if you still like her afterwards; she tells you so you can forge a proper connection. Her honesty allows you to also own your shit. Her acceptance of her true self forces you to stop burying the bits of yourself you don't like. It's an unnerving and empowering skill I'm not sure she even knows she possesses.

You'll know someone like this, someone you are magnetised towards because they are comfy in their skin. They are living their truest life and owning their shit. God, I love meeting people like this.

I ran from my truth for quite a few years and then, like most inauthentic things, being someone I wasn't became boring and hard work. The new, cooler, inauthentic you becomes normal and you yearn for something else. Luckily I stopped looking for other people's definitions of cool and settled on just being me. So much less draining. I think it's brilliant to try new things and challenge yourself in ways that feel fresh and exciting, but I don't believe creating a new look or persona for yourself will negate pain, problems or past trauma. For that you need to be YOU! I learned this every time I dyed my hair a new colour or got a new tattoo: I might have looked different on the outside, but I still had all the same insecurities and worries inside. You really can't run from your truth. It'll always catch you up.

QUITTING SELF-LOATHING AND DROPPING THE MIC

These days I understand that learning to like who I am is integral for me to live my truth, and vice versa. It's a tricky one, chicken and egg and all that. Which comes first? Maybe it doesn't matter, but perhaps one follows the other once you fully invest in either loving yourself or living your truth.

We all have moments of self-loathing and maybe you can recognise an inclination to swing towards self-loathing and doubt in certain situations. I would love to say I only occasionally find myself in situations in life that trigger such thought patterns, but I would BE LYING. I self-loathe all of the time. I could sit and point fingers and blame the outside judgement that I've had to get used to due to the nature of my job or the fact that I'm a classic perfectionist with all my stars sat in Virgo or I could remember that self-loathing is just a bad habit.

Some days, my lack of patience with my kids will set off a flare of it. On other days, the never-ending pit of anxiety that is my unanswered email inbox might be enough to kickstart it. Some days, the sight of my nose from the wrong angle; on others, a wrong turn down a traffic-filled road and a late drop-off to school. It could be anything. If you too dip into self-loathing regularly you might think this pattern of thought is set in stone; that perhaps it's 'just the way you are'. I think we all have the ability to change this negative self-talk with a little practice. After all, it's just a bad habit.

When I finish recording an episode of my Happy Place podcast I normally put the mic away, say goodbye to the guest with a hug and then spend at least thirty minutes thinking about all the things I should have done or said differently. On some days, this turns into me saying some pretty mean shit about myself, which isn't helpful at all. I think I often second-guess what the audience might say when they listen to the recording, so I try to get in there first with the troll-like comments and criticism. Maybe if I acknowledge the wrongs and mistakes first it won't hurt so bad when others say the same?

These days I understand that this self-criticism is not my truth, it is simply learned behaviour and that means I can unlearn it. At times, criticising myself has been a coping mechanism but it isn't my truth. It is unhelpful in every way and also starts to change what I believe about myself. The story slowly, incrementally, becomes, 'I am bad at this. I don't deserve to do this.'

We all know it takes great effort to learn a new skill – to perfect a piano piece, let a new language roll off the tongue, to balance in the most majestic yogic headstand – but what requires even more effort is unlearning. MY GAAAAD, unlearning is tough. We may have behaved in a certain way for years, decades, over half of our lifetime, so to 'unlearn' we need to be massively willing to look at ourselves. We need to get the magnifying glass out and really take note of what doesn't work for us anymore.

In those moments when I am picking myself apart after a podcast recording or press interview, am I enhancing my emotional or mental health in any way? Absolutely not. I'm wasting precious time worrying about something I can't change and that really doesn't matter. I'm allowing my fear of a future event that might not even happen, or the possible critique of people I do not know, to over-ride my own instincts and beliefs. During podcast recordings, or any other part of my job that I'm passionate about, I will always give it my best shot and do what feels right in the moment. All that really matters is that I tried my best and had good intent. I might still make mistakes, but I am human and that is inevitable. We all have to give ourselves the chance to try again without the debilitating self-loathing that can often creep up and stop us in our tracks. Wasting hours, or even days, mentally beating myself up about a past event does not serve me, so I have to look at new ways of rounding off events at work peacefully. Finding new ways means letting go of old habits.

Because I now recognise my tendency towards self-loathing and self-criticism as a behaviour I have learned, I understand that we can all take practical steps to implement new behavioural patterns and change how we feel about ourselves.

After each podcast episode, I now try to give myself some breathing space before the abuse begins in my head. If I feel the critical comments coming on, I try to think of the bits I loved during the episode – the parts of the conversation where it felt fluid and connected. This is not to be confused with complacency. I believe there is always room for improvement and learning but I can communicate this with myself in a much more nurturing and kind way with a little discipline and practice. I now try to say to myself, 'Maybe there were moments that could have been better, but you have another chance to try again on the next episode. Just enjoy where you are now.' This feels so much lighter and connects me to my truth: that I am someone with good intent, who is trying and ultimately wants to feel love – from my audience, from my guests but really love for myself.

Although our truth is founded in love, getting in touch with it might still be tricky to process and also to handle. The outcome might mean losing people from our lives, changing jobs, standing up to those who have previously dominated us, or saying NO for the first time. Change is hard. Few of us think we are good at change or feel comfortable in it but most of us thrive when we remember we are more than capable. It's just shit-scary at the time. It's why so many people stay in toxic relationships, jobs they hate, friendships that drain and mindsets that don't work anymore. It's much easier to stay put than go with change.

It might even be surprising to us when we work out the shape of our truth and recognise what changes we need to make. Again, it is scary because we have to look at our likes, dislikes, inclinations, sexuality, relationship dynamics, stress triggers and more to work out how we truly feel about life and ourselves. The truth isn't easy to look at because it requires acceptance, and sometimes action, but I think it is always a better option for a peaceful and honest life.

Can you excavate your own life to find your truth? Can you see beneath the stories you've told yourself, and told others, to see what is really pulsing in your heart? It might take months or even years of digging but it is in there waiting for permission to thrive. It lies in passion that makes your gut feel warm; it's white pure light that makes your bones feel light; it's strength as your feet root through Mother Earth's ground. It is there.

MY TRUTHS

- ★ A need for connection
- ★ A need for total solitude
- ★ A need for a slower pace
- ★ Being in a family
- ★ Pure love
- ★ A need for peace
- ★ A deep love of music
- ★ A constant desire to create
- ★ Time and space for myself
- ★ Eye contact
- ★ Feeling like I'm part of a movement or positive group
- ★ A dislike of parties and large groups
- ★ A dislike of feeling drunk or out of control
- ★ A need to move my body
- ★ A connection to nature and the outdoors
- ★ A love of feeding my body appropriately
- ★ Deep laughter
- ★ Listening

My truths

What truths do you need to remind yourself of?

_____

_____

_____

_____

_____

_____

_____

_____

_____

_____

_____

_____

_____

_____

_____

_____

_____

_____

_____

_____

_____

_____

4

HOW DO WE START SPEAKING OUT?

It is of course one thing to know our truth and another to start speaking it. We can work through our personal history and remove the lies and censors we've put on ourselves, but then we still have to find the confidence to stand up and speak it to others. How do we learn to roar again? How do we get back to realising we deserve to make sound and be heard?

I'm strangely better at speaking my truth on the big matters rather than the smaller, everyday stuff. Stick me in front of a crowd of strangers and ask me to talk about my mental health and the darkest moments of my life and I'm there! I will open my heart, be vulnerable, eloquent, honest and feel good doing it. I know my truth and am happy to share it. I don't feel judged in these situations because I'm not judging myself. I'm comfortable with most of the dark bits and know that each time I talk about them I'm relieved of a little more tension and worry. Yet ask me to deal with the possibility of everyday, unexpected conversations and I'm a quivering mess.

My absolute Achilles heel is people asking me for a favour. On text or email I have time to consider a response and explanation so I can set clear boundaries without embarrassment but in person I repeat the same mistake again and again. I get asked for a lot of favours and, to be clear, I don't mind at all as I want to help where I can but what I can't do is fulfil everything asked of me. Happy Place is a business I run with a team and this sits alongside my other jobs that involve design, writing, speaking publicly, etc. . . . and I'm raising my kids at the same time. Even though I know I'm very stretched, when someone asks me for something TO MY FACE (ahhhh, cornered) I always, ALWAYS say yes even when I know I have no time, energy or inclination. How shit is that!

My heart and gut screech to a halt and send a message to my brain and mouth to say, 'I won't be able to attend the opening of your local fete/judge your dog competition/ record a video for your aunty's birthday', yet my brain ignores all signals and starts my mouth moving into the shapes of the words 'OF COURSE'. I say it almost too emphatically in case they can tell I'm lying. I then often start talking about how I might go about what has been asked of me, what else I might be able to offer and by the end of the conversation, I've handed over my email address, asked if they want to go to dinner that night, if they might want to borrow one of my outfits to do so and then if they might like to use my car at the weekend. I can't stop myself!

Through writing this book I have been able to observe

this habit of mine and have found myself doing this at least three times already this month! WTF?! Agreeing to the request is bad, but this is where it gets ugly. There comes a time where I am then supposed to fulfil said request and I DON'T WANT TO. Not one bit of me can be bothered or has the time so then I get grumpy. I get pissed off at myself and then in turn with those around me who have nothing to do with the outcome of doing a favour. Sometimes I then have to painstakingly backtrack and extract myself from the situation or sometimes I go through with it with gritted teeth wishing I wasn't there. This is no good.

What would be better for everyone is a tactful 'no' right at the start. I find it soooo excruciating to do so. Partly because I'm a people pleaser and due to my strange job, I often assume everyone thinks I'm a moron from the get-go, so my ego wants to impress them and make them love me. And partly because I don't know how to choose the correct words to let someone down.

My husband is the best at this – the king of the Polite No. He is one of the friendliest people you'll meet, which helps. He knows the name of every dog walker, shopkeeper and barista on our local high street, which could lead to people feeling they could ask for things and cross the line easily. He is so clear with his boundaries that people rarely do but when this does occur he deals with it impeccably. I can only stand back, watch and learn.

Recently, on our way to grab a coffee, a man neither of us knew stopped us for a chat and said he knew some of Jesse's friends. He wanted to know if Jesse wanted to meet up and perhaps even play guitar with him. I instantly tensed up and wondered how the hell Jesse was going to deal with such an overt and out-of-the-blue ask. I was trying to telepathically send a signal to Jesse to give the guy a fake number. I mean, that's pretty 1990s of me! A fake number! Definitely did that back in the day in a few bars! No, instead Jesse very elegantly told the chap that he doesn't feel comfortable giving his number out to people he doesn't know well. A polite tip of the head and we were off for our morning caffeine hit unscathed. WOW! OK, that is how you deal with an awkward ask. I have to keep working at this so I don't end up flaking on people down the line or feeling resentful.

Me practising saying no is like watching a cat being shoved into a shower. I AM NOT COMFORTABLE with it. But this is how I'm trying – my god I'm trying. The first thing I need to remember when I'm put on the spot and asked for something is to breathe. If I breathe then I give my brain one more second to stop and think before I say, 'Of course I'll open your cousin's niece's friend's school fete!' I need that pause to think. I'm also thinking about the language I use a lot. I'm never going to be blunt or harsh with people because, as you've discovered, I'm way at the other end of the spectrum of people-pleasing, but I think looking at the language I use is helpful. I'm trying to start responses with little phrases like, 'That is so kind of you to think of me,' or, 'Thank you so much for asking me.' I'm experimenting with this one and have tried it out a little, as I mentioned at the very start of this book. It's getting a little easier but I have a LONG way to go. I'm trying out words like 'thank you' to initiate my turn-down, instead of beginning with an awkward and insincere apology. Then I pick through my vocabulary, carefully using phrases like 'I won't be able to' rather than 'I can't'. To me, 'won't' feels a little more responsible and illustrates that I have made the decision because I know what's best for me, rather than 'can't', which is usually a lie or a twist of the truth.

I am also trying to eliminate white lies, so no more 'I'm busy that night' or 'I'm working on that day' if I actually have a blank diary. I'm attempting to give the real reason as to why it's not right for me in a non-offensive way.

I've been practising relaying that I am slightly over-whelmed with work and family life so I'm at my own personal maximum capacity. No one can really argue with that as it's true and about my limits not theirs. One friend suggested I need not even give a reason. She says it is my right to say no and not discuss why, but I'm not quite there yet so giving a little personal tale of why I can't oblige makes me feel slightly more comfortable.

The aftermath of maintaining that boundary is up to me and that is an important point I have to remember. If the other in question has a problem with me saying no then that is their issue and not mine. I remind myself I am not to feel guilty as I have been honest and set a boundary. I am not to worry for hours afterwards whether they're pissed off or now view me differently as, again, that's not in my hands. I have to stay comfortable and strong in my own truth.

Of course, there are plenty of things I say yes to gleefully. Such as opportunities to help and be part of things that I know I can commit to without any resentment or worry about fatigue. The thing is, practising 'no' gives me the space to flex the 'yeses'.

BAD HAIR AND OPINIONS

During the process of writing this book I've also started to look at how I receive the truth. Am I good when others are honest with me? The answer is both yes and no. Recently, someone in my life got very real with me because they felt that a lot had been unspoken in our dynamic and it was causing issues between us. It was true, there was a huge lack of communication going on and we were both making assumptions about each other left, right and centre, which was affecting our relationship. What might have felt like a very awkward, tricky chat a few years ago actually felt very liberating and left us both with a sense of clearance and space. I was grateful to them for raising this directly with me when I know it would have been much easier to just seethe in silence instead. We ended our conversation with a lot more respect for one another and a renewed connection formed from empathy and listening to each other speak honestly.

Yet I also know at times when others speak their truth I get very judgey. I have been brought up by a tenacious and hard-working mum and a very chilled-out, polite, hard-working dad. Neither would dream of asking for anything in life. Anything they have they've worked for and earned and nothing is ever expected or demanded. I'm not sure if it's a generational thing but most of my relatives of this age would never dream of asking for something or owing someone. I've watched my mum and aunty have near fights over who pays the bill after a small lunch of a soup and sandwich in a cafe, both desperately wanting to pay and be the one who gives and doesn't receive. I've grown up with strong characters around me making stuff happen without help, so I often go about my business in the same way.

When I am faced with someone who has a more relaxed attitude to asking for something that I feel they haven't earned, my initial reaction can be a little eyebrow-raising and huffy. Because I don't ask for help I can get judgemental when others do. It's taken me some time to realise that's my hang-up and not theirs. If your truth starts to sound like judging others, it's always a good idea to look at yourself first. My truth, at times, might involve me requesting help or having to ask for a favour, so I need to get over this old belief of mine.

I'm also not good when people tell me what they think of me or offer an opinion that feels personal. There's a funny thing that happens when you're in the public eye where you become slightly dehumanised and people forget that you're a real person with feelings that can be hurt. For example, sometimes people who I know, or know a bit, make passing comments like, 'Your hair looked weird on the coverage of William and Kate's wedding.' (I know, it was so long ago and I STILL REMEMBER THE COMMENT! Note to self: must move on.) Or they tell me what they think I should be doing in my career.

I'm not always great at receiving this sort of opinion, however well-intentioned it might be. Initially I'll feel a surge of resentment, yet rather than challenge what's being said, I stay quiet and nod. I've realised that if I really want to speak my truth to others, I need to look at how I receive information from those who are perfectly confident in delivering it. Maybe I can give it a shot too – without judgement!

FAMILY LIFE AND AN IMPORTANT GRAIN OF RICE

To have well-oiled relationships that run smoothly and avoid drama we have to speak up. We need balance, understanding and, of course, boundaries. Establishing these requires a healthy dose of communication, as we don't get them all clearly outlined and explained in a relationship rule book and we can't read each other's minds, no matter how close we might be.

Jesse and I have had to get really good at communicating with each other, as from the off there were kids involved. Becoming a step-parent is a complicated process that starts long before you actually get married. From the moment you meet your partner's children from a previous marriage or relationship, you are responsible for some of their wellbeing and also how you navigate family life together. There was a time at the beginning of this new relationship when I felt I didn't have the right to say too much. Without kids of my own, I felt my main job was to be compliant and respect the arrangements that were in existence before I was involved.

There is a strange period of uncertainty when you enter a pre-existing family. A limbo land where your personal opinion seems less important as you all find your feet together. The kids, of course, are the priority as you are all trying to help them feel stable throughout a lot of change, but it is also important you find your own happiness and enjoy the fruits of a brand-new, exciting relationship. At the beginning of my relationship with Jesse, I started parking my own opinions and comfort in this new family set-up as I was young and inexperienced in speaking up. Most of my relationships prior to meeting Jesse had failed due to a lack of communication, usually from me, which led to great resentment on all sides.

After a year with Jesse, I fell pregnant and, from deep within me, my motherly instinct needed to speak up. From the first few weeks of pregnancy, where Rex was the size of a grain of rice, I felt this insatiable need to have my say. I now felt I had a proper place in this newly blended family. It shouldn't have taken me getting pregnant to feel this, as I already did have my place, but for me it took this significant moment to help with change. I had a little grain of rice with a beating heart that needed looking after, and two stepchildren who needed support in getting used to even more change. I started to believe that I deserved a say in how the cogs of family life turned as my truth was shouting a lot louder. It was all new – a small pot belly, a new-found confidence and the need to speak up, even if it did rock the boat a little.

I must add that Jesse is the least pushy person out there and would never impose any kind of family values or rules upon me and that's always been the case. This lack of communication came purely from my own insecurity and meant I let Jesse and the existing arrangements take the lead. This was a situation that had to change. We were about to have our own baby son and we could no longer work to a rhythm in which my voice was excluded. I had to speak up. Quite simply, I needed to put my own needs and rules in place as we changed the shape and size of our family.

At first, speaking up was difficult and at times I roared

way too loud, usually in Jesse's direction. Years of pent-up suppression led to occasional anger as I finally allowed myself to say how I felt. It was a liberation that I felt foolish to have not exercised previously. If I needed to say something to Jesse or the children at this time, I would usually feel hot and flushed beforehand and my heart would race uncontrollably as my physical body prepared for rejection or humiliation. In the early days of establishing my own needs in our family life, I would caveat every opinion with, 'If it's OK with you lot, I would like . . .' or, 'I know it might not be ideal but . . .' Nine years down the line, and through a lot of practice, I find it easier to say my bit and get my point across without sounding unsure or apologetic. I know I have a proper place in this family unit and it's important I let the words escape my mouth. To find balance and harmony we all need the space to say our bit.

If speaking up feels scary, remember that not speaking up can be worse, leading to resentment, anger and usually an explosion of frustration later on over something small and insignificant. Jesse hasn't rejected me in these moments where I speak up; my step-kids haven't turned against me. The kids may feel pissed off for a second when I'm wanging on about dirty towels on floors or front doors slamming at midnight not being appropriate but I'm OK with that. It is more important that I speak my truth than it is to keep everyone else happy the whole time.

If you are a step-parent you'll know it feels tricky to establish how you might use discipline within the home. You might feel it's not your place to tell your stepchildren that you don't like them using their phones at the table or leaving mounds of washing on the floor but it is imperative to give them boundaries to establish a healthy relationship with mutual respect. I also think it helps the longevity of that relationship as the conversation is explicitly open for you and them.

If you want to hear this subject in depth, check out the episode of Happy Place I recorded with Rio and Kate Ferdinand. They speak so eloquently about blended families and learning to speak up. Rio's first wife died of breast cancer leaving him bereft and with three young, grieving children to look after. Down the line, he met and later married Kate, who willingly took on the role of stepmother overnight, knowing she was not only taking on three kids, she was also stepping into a lot of grief. Rio and Kate made a brilliant documentary about step-parenting and grief called *Becoming a Stepfamily*. I was so struck by how wonderfully honest all members of the family were on screen and exhaled with relief that there were real conversations on mainstream TV about the challenges of having a blended family. I think many of us have been trying to banish the archaic notion of 'the evil stepmother' for some time, but I'll still get pissed off reading my kids stories that feature that very character in 2020! Kate Ferdinand managed to enter a grieving family and not only help them all find comfort and support but also set her own rules to create comfort for herself. Now that I was in awe of.

She gradually felt the need to have conversations with Rio about changing parts of the family home that felt very tied to a life Kate hadn't been part of. For her to feel at home and comfortable she needed to make her own mark on their living space and within the family dynamic. She did this all with utter grace and explained every step of the way to the kids. No fallout, no label of evil stepmum and a whole heap of honesty.

In the podcast, we cover all aspects of step-parenting and blended families so if you're in the same boat, head on over to Happy Place. Though, of course, being honest and setting boundaries applies to any family set-up, not just blended ones.

KEEPING QUIET AND TOO MUCH AFTERSHAVE

Within my working life I have found speaking my truth so tricky at times. Mad, considering I talk for a living. That's literally all I used to do. TALK!

At the start of my career, I didn't dare say a word. I was the new kid on the block; I was the suburban scruffbag without a clue. Big-eyed and willing to learn, I didn't want to ruffle any feathers at all.

'Wear those awful purple corduroy trousers on live TV' you say? SURE!

'Be dementedly enthusiastic about presenting a kids' cartoon even though you're sixteen and the only TV you watch is *Neighbours*' you say? OF COURSE!

I would never have dared speak up even though the people I worked with were kind and very loving. I'm so lucky that I started my career under the watchful eye of two of the best bosses ever. Maddy Darrall and Billy Macqueen nurtured me and Reggie Yates and the other *Disney Club* kids of the 1990s, making sure we kept on the straight and narrow and felt comfortable with what we were doing at all times. I owe them everything. To this day I refer back to the comfort and support they offered in the work environment, yet I have rarely found it in adult life. Their example is one of my main motivations today in creating a career and company that feels kind. Looking back, some of that restraint served me well as I kept my job, which led to other great opportunities, but down the line I think I would have done myself a huge favour by speaking the hell up.

In my early twenties, I was offered a big TV job that I initially wasn't keen on. I had been offered an even bigger show by the same powerful, clichéd, strong-aftershave-wearing man a short time before, only for him to then give it to someone else without telling me. So when the next offer came in from him, I wanted to say 'NO!' How could I work for this person who had lied to me so blatantly? My dignity and truth said no but I still took the job out of fear of not working again. So many of my decisions were based on fear, back in the day (NOT ANYMORE, SUCKERS!).

I started the new job and felt a low-level resentment building up within me. Another producer, lower down in the TV hierarchy than Mr Aftershave, came up with wacky ideas and over-the-top moments that would set our show apart from others. I felt uncomfortable with these ideas as I wanted to leave the kids' TV persona behind now I was in my twenties. I could handle my mates and others taking the piss out of my fluorescent clothing and my wide-screen TV grin at the age of eighteen, but I wasn't a teenager anymore and I was over it.

I felt an internal tension when having to film these cheesy pieces to camera. I couldn't fully let go and commit to what was being asked of me as it felt inherently wrong. My truth was telling me no but I was too scared to speak up. Mouth shut. Smile on. Appropriate clothing ('Can you look more like Cat Deeley?'). Words spoken on camera like a good girl. Yet none of it aligned with the truth.

I finished up on the series without seeing the 'big boss' much at all but, after it had come to an end, I heard from my agent that, while the show was returning the next year, Mr Aftershave had decided I wouldn't be. Put more plainly: I was sacked. Relief churned with embarrassment. I had never wanted to do the show or felt aligned with how it was presented. Why hadn't I spoken up? Out of fear of being thought of as cocky, perhaps? Or maybe a fear that my ideas wouldn't be as good as theirs?

Now I am writing this book, I have the opportunity to question what would have happened if I had spoken up. What shit would have gone down if I had spoken my truth? Maybe the producer coming up with the ideas would have argued their creative point? Maybe we could have had a big, juicy conversation about all of it? Maybe they would have had more respect for me for speaking up? Maybe I would have been left feeling less humiliated afterwards? There are so many possible outcomes and I probably would have stopped doing the show regardless but at least I would have known that I had spoken up and honoured my truth.

I would love to tell you that the part of my career where I am treated like an ephemeral, disposable commodity is over but it's not. I was 'taken off' another show in a similar way more recently and it always feels slightly painful. Not your gut-wrenching, cry-your-eyes-out pain, more of a 'I've stubbed my toe really badly and everyone saw me do it' pain. Being treated as if you are disposable makes you feel throwaway. When you're easily replaced on a job it can be hard to remember your own strengths as others clearly don't see or value them.

In the industry I work in, as in many others out there, people are often treated as numbers. They try you out, push you around the chess board a little, try to fit you into their game and how they want it to look – and if you don't fit, well, it's checkmate, you're off the board. It's one of the reasons that I have worked so hard to forge my own path in life where I am not sat constantly begging at the feet of a TV boss to not just hire me but like me too. It's too painful to repeat that again and again and keep your self-worth in check.

There is a real lack of creativity working in that way too, and my main driving force in life is creativity. Creativity is my joy! It's my gin and tonic, my sunset, my hot bath on a cold day, my drop of the beat. I thrive when I'm being creative and in most of the jobs where I have been disposable there is so little creativity afoot that I feel flat before I've even started. I cannot tell you how lucky I feel to even be writing this book. Blank page after blank page of space for me to create. I feel overjoyed every time I get to research and start a new podcast episode, creating and cultivating conversation for others to hear. And the best bit? No one can sack me. People can choose to not engage with my work but I can't be treated like a commodity. What a sodding relief!

ONE MORE TIME WITH FEELING

Years and years of experience and confidence-building have enabled me to feel confident enough to say my bit when it comes to my work. If I feel uncomfortable with an idea being put forward to me, I will always say what I believe is right. Although, wait . . . the other day, just last week, I didn't do this. A hang-over moment. A one-off situation where I was tired from parenting and run-down from too little sleep and eating on the run.

There was some filming I wasn't that into that I was too tired to say no to. I'm perhaps not that easy to direct these days as I feel confident in who I am and what my truth is at work, and reluctant to change it to fit someone else's idea of what's best. One of my least favourite bits of direction is to be told to give it some more energy. I was told for so many years through my twenties to 'give it more energy', even when the way I was delivering the piece to camera felt natural to me. Someone from behind a camera or down my earpiece would holler, 'Go on ONE MORE TIME, with MORE energy.' PISS OFF with your energy; I simply don't have any more. So, last week, as a thirty-nine-year-old woman, I acted like a child. I was mopey and quiet and rushed through what I was supposed to do. It didn't feel good at the time and I felt regretful afterwards and vowed never to reject my gut feeling again.

During the writing of this book, I have looked at these slip-ups more intently and with curiosity. I have asked myself why I didn't speak. I have examined the fallout from staying silent. I have looked at what other outcomes might have been possible. Self-inventory in these moments is the only option if we really want to grow.

My work today mainly revolves around a big, beautiful team of people who help me bring the Happy Place business to life. It's not just a podcast; we are putting on festivals, developing charity initiatives, and creating new ways to talk about mental health. My work life has changed so much from what it used to be. In the Happy Place business meetings I'm more than happy to speak up as there is too much riding on it if I don't. Things I care about greatly might go wrong, decisions could be made that I feel uncomfortable with and that could affect many others. Passion usually helps drive honesty as you can see the potential fallout if you're not truthful. When you care less about things, sometimes it is easier to be sloppy. I'm working towards having integrity in all areas of my life, no matter how big or small.

CONFIDENCE AND TWITCHY LEGS

If you experience any level of success from speaking your truth it can act as an instant confidence boost. If you have told your partner that you don't like it when she/he talks over you and that is received with understanding and establishes a new dynamic, you may feel you can speak openly in other areas of your life. If you have managed to summon the strength to tell your boss you feel overwhelmed by your workload and it was met with empathy and a positive change in your role, you may feel you can flex this muscle in other areas too. If you don't give it a go you'll never know.

Jesse and I are big communicators who now have many lengthy discussions to try to find peaceful pockets so our busy family life and work lives can work cohesively. Initially, though, we would both approach tricky situations with a lack of confidence or, like I said previously, not say anything at all. Over time and with practice, we have gotten much better at asking things of each other, telling each other how we feel and also asking for change. Because we've had successful communication and honesty in these moments, it's opened up more opportunity for it to happen again.

Jesse has confronted me about situations he thinks need addressing and, although at first we may fight and shout in a knee-jerk reaction, we know we'll ultimately find some peace down the line. And I've been able to broach tricky subjects with Jesse and know that we will find compromise or a middle ground that works for us both.

Confrontation can create extreme physical fear and paralysis in situations where the result of speaking up is uncertain. In most moments of confrontation, I have a racing heart, darting eyes and legs as twitchy as a sleeping dog. This physical reaction does not create stability when trying to speak one's truth.

On a practical note, I think there are a few things we can do to get ourselves ready for practising speaking our truth. I've learned some techniques to train our unruly bodies to help us deliver words clearly and confidently. If you know you want to have a potentially difficult chat with a friend, work colleague or member of your family, can you give yourself some prep time? Perhaps an hour in a quiet space where you can practise.

Pretend they are there in front of you. Experiment with what the words feel like when they leave your mouth and how they sound once they hit the air. If there is anger, resentment or a power play present, can you root back to that inner truth and love and find the best words for this situation? The correct words which will allow you to be heard and get what you need out of the dynamic but also ones that will keep the peace? I often ask a mate (hey, Clare Bennett!) to help me with this as I can get too sucked into anger and a ranty tone if I'm not careful. A mate who you trust will have a more impartial stance on the matter to help you almost script this moment.

Think of what the person's responses might be and imagine how you might feel if the things you want to say were said to you. But don't think up the worst-case scenario straight away. Think optimistically: might they receive the news, question or statement well and with understanding? Imagine how you might address any concerns, worries or fears the other person has.

Keep your truth in mind; what you deserve and what you know you need. Never let this falter because, as soon as you do, there is room for error in what you say. I know if I lose sight of what I initially set out to achieve, I will start to backtrack and apologise. And then I start contradicting myself entirely. It is important that we are fully confident in our own truth before we start to speak it. If there is any uncertainty in our tone of voice or delivery, that is when others may take advantage, twist our words or not listen properly. Other people know uncertainty. They can sense it.

You may have listened to someone uncertain of their truth

speaking and thought about how wobbly their statements were. Maybe you were unsure whether to believe them or connect with them fully because they seemed too unsure. For the other person or group in the dynamic to listen properly and to act on what you are saying it's important you communicate confidently. This may not feel natural to you – maybe you believe you are a shy person who cannot stand up for themselves. But our personalities are not fixed; we have the ability to change if we think it'll benefit our lives.

A lot of confidence is practice. Yes, some are perhaps born or brought up with a little more confidence in how they speak up but a lot of it is learned too. I did not start off in this career feeling confident, yet each time I showed up for work I knew I had another go at mastering my conviction of speech. I'm still in that process now.

In any situation where we have to explain ourselves, ask something of another or simply tell the world who we are, remember not to be scared of silence. If the other person is digesting what you've just said or having a pause to think, don't fill the gap. That is when you're most likely to say something that doesn't align with your truth. If you're like me, you'll want to make the other person feel comfortable and will squeeze words into that silent pause. And they might not be the best-chosen words. Let the silence drift in and out with the same confidence that is holding your truth.

If we have given ourselves some practice time we might now feel more acquainted with our own opinion and voice. Maybe we now feel confident enough to release the words into the wild. This is where my nerves often get the better of me. My shoulders tense and my face goes beetroot. Breathing is key. It may sound obvious but let the breath help push these words out. Let the breath keep your body soft and fluid. Deep breaths tell the body that it is relaxed. With constant deep breathing we can lower our heart rate and calm our nervous system so we stay on track with what we are feeling and what we need to say.

My great friend Rebecca Dennis has helped me massively with breathwork. Her work as a breath coach has helped so many people move through trauma, reduce their anxiety and bring confidence into the picture. The key to it all is a simple inhalation followed by an exhalation. So often we forget to breathe at all, so keeping it at the forefront of our minds at times where we feel nervous is important if we want to deliver information confidently.

Remember your stance and posture. Are you delivering your message with back hunched and fingers fumbling? Have you contorted your body so it is folded in and small? Remember to stand straight, head high, chest out, arms wide. Take up as much room as you deserve. You deserve to be here and you deserve to take up space. As I am writing this, I am reminding myself of this too. You're not going to do this in an intimidating way to impose a gorilla-like dominant energy in the room, you're merely understanding your own worth and how you deserve to stand proudly, saying your bit. If I have to do public speaking I have to really bear this in mind.

I once hosted the Mind Media Awards on behalf of the mental health charity Mind, and the inimitable Stephen Fry was sitting in the front row next to the Duke of Sussex, Prince Harry. I MEAN, how much pressure? Initial thoughts: what the hell am I doing on this stage? This shouldn't be allowed! Why am I up here talking in the company of such distinguished guests? Remembering my own worth and truth was imperative in this moment and I had to physically show it. I couldn't slope onto the stage with my shoulders curved towards the floor and a timid gaze to match. I had to stride, sparkly shoes leading the way to the podium where I would seem so at home with my broad shoulders straight and aligned and my feet set apart.

Leading with body confidence works, it gives you that extra push towards the true confidence that you need. My head might not have been 100 per cent on board with believing I was worthy and deserved to be on that stage, but my body language said I felt extremely confident all round and my head slowly caught up with the idea the longer I held the stance. I've never been let down by this one. It's as if your body leads and then your brain and mouth get the memo.

REMEMBER WHEN YOU WERE LAST SCARED

Even with all of these pointers, speaking out might still seem way too scary and far out of your comfort zone. If so, try to remember the last time you faced a fear. What was it? How did it feel in the moment that you pushed past the fear and did it anyway? Usually way less scary than you had imagined, right?

I had an absurd fear to deal with recently that took me by surprise. I was booked to be a guest on *Sunday Brunch*, which I've had the pleasure of doing a few times over the years. I was due to go on, have a chat and then cook up one of the dishes from my book, *Happy Vegan*. For some reason, the night before I went into utter panic. What if I don't say anything interesting? What if I cock up the dish on LIVE TV? What if I swear or say something stupid? I'm out of practice when it comes to appearing on other people's shows as I spend so much time now making my own programming via my podcast. I didn't sleep a wink. Pure panic and a lot of wasted energy. I got out of bed groggily at 5:30 a.m. and headed to the studio. Make-up covered my grey eyes and some lovely producers and food prep team members calmed my nerves.

Was it as scary and awful as I had imagined? Of course not! I had a right laugh, made vegan sausages that were widely appreciated by all in the studio and got a free cocktail before midday to boot. Relief!

This post-achievement confidence lasts a little while but, like with anything, it's a muscle that needs to be flexed regularly to work with ease. It's the same with speaking our truth. The more we speak our truth the easier it gets. The more we get used to being listened to. The more we realise we are worthy of being listened to. Is that perhaps a subconscious insecurity you have? That you do not deserve to be listened to? Maybe, when growing up, you weren't listened to at home or school. Maybe you believe that every time you speak people tune out or that they don't see validity in what you're saying. That is not true at all. It's just all learned behaviour, so you can unlearn it. You have a lot to say and it IS worthy of being listened to.

If you're doubting this, think of all the rubbish we've

consumed on TV, or the lies we've been told by politicians; do those people have more to offer the world than you? Of course not, they just had a lot of confidence in speaking (not necessarily truthfully). So much of speaking up and speaking our truth comes down to confidence. Some of us have oodles of the stuff (some have too much), some have too little, some of us feel we once had it but it's been taken from us (ME! ME!) but we can all practise. Like any skill, practice creates ease and confidence – so get out there and get started. The first few times you may be wobbly and you might even get thrown off track believing it's not for you, but don't be deterred. Think about what the other option is: a life of resentment and built-up frustration, never really saying what you feel. We all deserve to speak out loud and we all deserve to be heard.

MAKE SOME NOISE

Not long after I received the diagnosis of a throat cyst, I picked up my trusty, battered copy of Louise Hay's *Heal Your Body* (I urge you to get this manual about how self-love is the root to all healing). I opened it and looked up the entry for 'throat'. This book lists every physical ailment possible and tells you the cause (usually emotion) and then the affirmation to practise. This one rang TRUE! Next to throat in this wondrous book Louise writes: 'Throat Problems: The inability to speak up for one's self. Swallowed anger. Stifled creativity. Refusal to change.'

Eeee, another confirmation that my cyst might be entirely

made up of stifled words and suppression. The affirmation Louise suggested that I had to now live by was: 'It's OK to make noise. I express myself freely and joyously. I speak up for myself with ease. I express my creativity. I am willing to change.' YES, this was it. Thank you, Louise Hay. It is OF COURSE OK to make noise.

So often we think we have to be quiet or silent because we don't want to upset others; perhaps we even fear we'll be punished. I had forgotten it was OK to make noise. I had absolutely forgotten it was OK to stand up for myself. I assumed other people's opinions were much more valid than my own. But wait, don't I know ME better than other people do?! Don't I see others making a hell of a lot of noise? This whole episode with my throat has allowed me to remember it is safe, and OK, to make noise.

When I gave birth to Honey I had chosen to have a water birth. On arrival at the hospital, things were running smoothly with my labour so I was able to do as I had wished. At first the contractions were manageable and I was able to breathe through this experience in a calm and silent way. Jesse had put little tea lights around the edge of the birthing pool and I stayed serene and calm. At one point, as things intensified, I flipped over onto all fours. There was no thought, this was animalistic instinct. I could feel the baby moving down, preparing to enter the world.

I roared. A low, earthy tone filled the room. I was loud. Jesse stood back, the midwife watched on. Howling, releasing an ancient female energy that has helped create life for aeons. More roaring, so loud, without care. I felt safe. Safe to make noise and safe to roar. I felt powerful, in the moment, connected to life and the source of all love. Noise felt natural. I knew it would help. It matched the intensity of what was physically taking place and enabled me to help the baby into the world. Honey glided into the pool with my last almighty roar. She was silent. Peaceful and serene with a shock of red hair but with an understanding that it is OK to make noise.

Where could you make more noise
in your life?

_____

_____

_____

_____

_____

_____

_____

_____

Where are you too silent?

_____

_____

_____

_____

_____

_____

_____

_____

_____

5

WHAT IF PEOPLE DON'T WANT TO HEAR IT?

How many times have you swallowed down words? How often have you pushed them to the base of your throat without any chance of escape? Added them to the graveyard of squashed syllables and broken sentences? I know that I have stood nodding when really inside I have disagreed. I have also said things like, 'Oh yes, I have seen that film and loved it,' even though I have never heard of it. I have let others speak over me and trample my words, one by one, into the ground, believing their opinion is more valid than my own. I know that every time I have silenced myself it is because of fear. A deep-rooted, subliminal fear of what the people around me will think. How will my truth be judged?

While I've been writing this book many strange, coincidental events have taken place to really open my eyes and make me look at why I get so scared of what other people think.

WhatsApp group chats are my nemesis. I always get so behind in the constant torrent of messages. Pings and words jolt my body into high alert, and the more behind I become the less I want to look. Just before the pandemic, I thought another mum from the school had messaged me privately, what I hadn't noticed was that the message was in the WHOLE CLASS group. The lovely mum in question had asked if I could make an event she was putting on that Saturday. I typed back with one thumb doing the work while the other hand stirred a pot of soup on the hob.

> Thanks so much for the invite, lovely, I can't make it though because I'm taking Rex and a few of the lads from the class bowling for his birthday. I can't be doing with this invite-the-whole-class-to-a-party thing anymore. Have a great time anyway. Much love.

Then, five minutes later, I checked to see if she had responded and then noticed the 'class PP2' title above our messages. FUCK! I have just told the rest of the mums that I don't want to entertain their kids anymore. A subliminal message of 'even if I do accept an invitation to your brilliantly arranged WHOLE CLASS party, you won't be coming to mine'. Shit bags!

'Jesse, Jesse, guess what I've done. Why am I so bad at phones? Why do I rush everything?'

Jesse's response is always the same: 'Who cares?'

At this point, I get slightly uptight and pink in the face.

'ME! Me, I care! They'll all hate me.'

But then, minutes later, I remember I'm in the middle of writing this book. This book on TRUTH! I didn't lie, I was honest, I was simply saying how I felt. Is that so bad?

Will everyone else hate me? Maybe some other mums will breathe a sigh of relief that the pressure's off inviting the whole class to their kid's party? Who knows – and, indeed, who cares? The ones who like me still will and if there are any who don't, I needn't worry about them anyway.

THE FEAR OF BEING ALONE AND CREATING BOUNDARIES

We often believe speaking our truth will lead to rejection but is this fear rational? If we say our bit and tell people how we really feel, will we really end up alone? This has often been my fear and it's frequently led me to not speak my truth at all.

In the past, I have been bad at setting boundaries early on in relationships, so have ended up in a place of chaos, confusion and usually resentment. For many years, I would moan the same moans to eye-rolling friends as I was blind to the pattern I was creating from relationship to relationship. We usually need to pull focus and see the scenario with a little distance to recognise the negative patterns we are repeating. Sometimes it takes a big one – one almighty shit storm, a Mount Vesuvius of pain – for us to really get the point and learn the lesson.

I had one particular working dynamic completely break down because I failed to speak up and be honest early on in the relationship. I was scared that my truth would make the other person flee. I was worried about asking too much and that if I expressed my needs I would then be punished or treated badly. A strange belief considering I'm not religious and don't believe in condemnation. This dynamic was no different to every other time I've started a friendship or relationship without boundaries. It just felt bigger. I needed to learn the lesson properly, so it happened again but in a much more dramatic and upsetting way.

Due to my strange job, I often go above and beyond in wanting others to see me as friendly and mostly, well, normal. I don't want to be thrown into the mythical group of 'celebrities' with all of the clichés that implies, as I don't feel that word describes me at all. I desperately want people to understand me and see that I'm much more 'comfy socks and strong coffee' than 'red-soled shoes and champagne'. Not that there is anything wrong with the other option, it's just not me. I want to show people that you can have this weird job, be in the public eye, yet still have a normal home and social life. This is my truth these days and I'm desperate to show it. I have an insatiable need to take back the normality that disappeared from my life in my twenties. I'm constantly reminding myself that the myths of this industry don't exist and that all the normal stuff is the best bit. I want others to see this too. I think this need has been exacerbated more recently due to how people view fame as a kind of magical cure for sorrow and shame. There's a sense that fame will create more sparkle and sheen in one's life. From personal experience, fame has offered me very little. I've been in the public eye since my mid-teens and it's only served up a heavy portion of paranoia and way too much self-analysis.

Success is the thing that has allowed me opportunity.

To me, fame equals the odd shout of, 'Oi, Fearne Cotton!' or sometimes it's, 'Oi, Fern Britton!' and that is it, there's not much more to it. Yet success has allowed me so much. It has given me the chance to write this very book. It has given me years of experience to build on and keep creating. It's stretched me to try new things and unlock parts of myself I didn't know existed. I don't see success as some shiny trophy you hold aloft to dominate others or to mitigate challenges, I see it as opportunity. After years of working in one industry I now have certain opportunities because I've gained experience, confidence and an understanding of my own strengths.

I have worked hard, tried new things, had some luck thrown in here and there and that has allowed me more freedom at work and the opportunity to meet and collaborate with wonderful people. Anyway, I digress, my point is that, as you can imagine, proving how normal and relatable I am has become somewhat of a subconscious drive when I meet new people.

I started this particular working relationship by trying to show this a little too passionately. My truth was that I needed someone to help me and should have set boundaries and given clear guidance as to what my needs were, but I didn't because I was too busy trying to express how lovely and giving I was.

As the years passed, the dynamic became strained and a huge canyon appeared where silence reigned and thoughts festered. I started to witness behaviour I had allowed yet didn't like one bit. Resentments grew as the words slipped away and the responses on both sides became exaggerated.

I gave more, was even more lenient and didn't speak up; the other person involved took more, asked for more and spoke up regularly. I was the one who had created this dynamic and I was now the one suffering.

Further down the line, it all imploded in a five-minute conversation. When I finally spoke up, and said a long-overdue no, the other person was shocked and claimed they had never been treated so badly. Because I hadn't said no before, they saw my behaviour as unkind and lacking in generosity. My truth landed heavily because I hadn't articulated it early on. I hadn't specified my boundaries and what I was capable of and willing to work with. My refusal to continue the previously established dynamic was met with confusion and then anger. Years of pent-up words and frustrations ended in a short, heated discussion and a dramatically slammed door.

I was left reeling for months, wondering how I could have done things differently and what the outcome would have been if I had been honest from the start. The relationship would, of course, have had a very different feel to it if I had gotten over my fear of being judged in the initial moments of working together. I would have established boundaries and clearly stated what would work for me. Instead, I gulped down words and let fear reign supreme.

Luckily, though, this story ends well. One rainy Tuesday, a letter was posted through our letterbox. It was a note of apology and an explanation that allowed me to release months of crinkled-forehead worry and jaw-tightening stress. I replied immediately, wishing nothing but good vibes and a clean slate as well as offering an apology of my own for having not been honest. We both desperately needed that moment to relieve us from a lot of pain and worry.

DON'T CATCH THE GUILT

When I think back to this situation, and other times where I have not spoken my truth, I like to imagine how it could have turned out had I spoken up and said what I really felt from the start. Would it have sounded rude if I had set boundaries on day one? Would I have ended up being labelled a terrible loudmouth? Could I have gotten over my belief that I don't deserve help and actually enjoyed asking for it?

This situation prompted me to take a closer look at why I had been so bad at communicating my truth and why for years this had been a pattern for me. While excavating the rubble that was left from this torpedoed working relationship, I learned several things. The first lesson is that I'm bloody awful at asking for help. I know this and see my behavioural patterns play out because of it. But I've also realised that we are not responsible for how another person reacts to our truth.

If we know that what we are saying is backed up by truth, good intent and thought, then the rest of the story is down to the other person involved. If the other party feels victimised or unfairly treated, yet you know that your reasons and beliefs align with the truth, then the other person's reaction is not to be carried upon your shoulders. Obviously if you are speaking your truth you needn't throw out vicious speech or have strong emotion behind your words. If you need to set boundaries, say no, ask for something or confront someone and your intent is good, then your delivery can be calm, kind and gentle. If we set the record straight with people from the start then there is little need for anger or upset because we have been clear. When I haven't been clear in certain friend-ship or family dynamics I find myself responding in a heavy way. My comments might be loaded with anger or spite because I know that I haven't previously been fully honest. When we know we have good intent then we always deliver our piece kindly. If you feel you have been treated badly and that kindness would be disingenuous, then of course that delivery can be neutral.

My point is that this isn't about firing off and saying whatever you want however you want without thought. It's about establishing healthy relationships through honesty, kindness and a little compassion. How the other person/people react is down to their view of the world and their personal history. If they have felt like a victim since childhood then victimhood is likely to be their reaction. If they haven't been told no before then maybe they won't be able to see another point of view or have empathy. If they have been brought up with strict rules maybe they struggle to be flexible. All we have to remember is that how someone else processes your truth is not your responsibility. Their reaction says much more about them than it does about you and your truth.

I remember once being told not to catch people's guilt. Guilt gets chucked around a lot and if it lands on you, it can really stop you in your tracks. It's an icky, hard-to-wash-off, heavy feeling that we have all dealt with on some level. You might stay in a relationship, job or friendship purely based on the guilt you feel. You might put off starting a hobby that intrigues you, never give yourself any downtime (ME!) or fail to speak up because you feel guilt. Guilt from the past, guilt from a present dynamic, guilt about how you might feel if you action that desire you've been suppressing.

Guilt isn't something we can feel alone – it always involves taking on other people's feelings. If we were alone and wanted to have downtime or to start a new venture we wouldn't feel guilty; it occurs when we start to think, 'But so-and-so might/will think . . .' or, 'No one else would be so lavish/selfish,' etc. Guilt relies on outside opinion – real or imagined – and the thing about outside opinion is, as we've established, it's not YOURS. So, the advice from the wise person I spoke with said to simply not catch it. If someone chucks it your way, keep your hands by your side. If you have a friend who always tells you they are disappointed when you don't get drunk with them, don't catch the guilt. Let it be theirs. If your aunt always mentions your lack of visits when you call, don't catch the guilt. If other mums seem to spend more time at home with their kids, or working, don't catch the guilt you feel they are projecting. There is no right or wrong option with any of these situations, only your truth and what is right for you.

My guilt always shows up in the form of feeling like I'm not doing enough or trying enough. When I look at that on paper I know it's a little bit crazy as I have four kids, a business, festivals in the summer to organise, books to write, podcasts to record, charities to work. And yet I catch the guilt from either other parents who don't work (who, by the way, would never want me to feel anything negative due to their circumstance or my own); my peers who seem to work harder or for longer hours; and from those who have fewer opportunities than I do. I feel I have to prove myself to a mythical all-seeing character who is supposedly judging me from the outside and therefore dishing out a big plate of guilt. I have to remind myself that the one judging me here is me! I need to keep my arms by my sides and not catch my guilt. My truth looks different to those around me so I have to focus on that instead.

HEALTHY DEBATE AND AWKWARD SILENCE

The British national characteristic of 'politeness at all costs' gets massively in the way of truth. Sometimes there is nothing better than just getting stuck into a big, juicy and perhaps heated discussion. I have learned time and time again that it's usually much healthier to get heated and have a debate rather than being polite through gritted teeth. I'm not sure many other nations do passive-aggressive like us Brits. We are the masters at not speaking up but then clenching our fists behind our backs in irritation that we haven't been understood. We are experts in 'the Look' – you know, the look that says, 'I cannot believe you're not reading my mind right now. How can you not tell I am furious?' yet never actually saying a word out loud. We say yes when really we mean no and then waste hours, weeks, even years building up resentment that will no doubt explode out of us at some point in the future. We are a funny old bunch.

It must hark back to our great-grandparents or grandparents who lived through the hell of war so built up an emotional armour to cope and protect themselves. A word most would use to describe Britishness is 'stoic'. We might not individually feel stoic but we know the post-Second World War generation were, the Queen most definitely is and, by osmosis, it has seeped into our culture in so many ways. Sometimes that stoicism gets warped and turns into keeping a stiff upper lip and not expressing our emotions, which never does anyone any good. Has the incredible stoicism that was used as a much-needed coping mechanism perhaps mutated over the years into an inability to discuss how we really feel?

It isn't always rude or unkind to be honest. The idea that honesty is rude has evolved in our culture into a feeling that it is safest and best to stick to the rules of this dance we call conversation. The unspoken rules that state we must ask about the weather, not cause a scene and mustn't endure silence for longer than two seconds.

I was chatting recently with my friend, the great Norwegian explorer and expert on all things silence, Erling Kagge. He told me that the Japanese have many more moments of silence within their conversations and daily lives than we do in Western cultures. We have become so conditioned by generations of belief that we must adhere to how conversation 'should' be carried out that we've forgotten there is another way.

I often have very heated debates with my dad – never actual arguments as he is far too mild-mannered and reasonable for that, even when I'm being a brat. We discuss politics, the environment, influential people and other big world topics from very different standpoints. I'm all 'emotions on my fluorescent sleeve' whereas dear Mick Cotton might cry at the sight of a newborn puppy but would never want to talk to you about it afterwards. I'm a heavy ball of emotions followed by a flurry of words whereas the big MC is watery-eyed and beautifully connected to emotions without explanation. We deal with stress differently, upset differently, anger differently. When I say 'differently' I can succinctly summarise how: I shout and wail about it; he calmly takes a step back, thinks and doesn't act out. He is the epitome of calm and I so appreciate that.

We differ in what we like in other areas too. I am often naively optimistic and full of praise for others whereas my dad is more sceptical and in need of hard facts before he makes up his mind about someone. I'm all party-popper-celebratory about other people whereas he is curious from afar. We know this about each other which makes things easier. We kind of know what we are going to get from a discussion. We chat it out, see each other's views, sometimes challenge each other, but it feels healthy. He is one person with whom I know that even if we can't see eye-to-eye we can have fun trying and also there will be no burnt bridges afterwards.

I have previously been incredibly honest with friends when I felt it was the right and decent thing to do. One friend had broken up with a partner and, whenever we met, recycled old arguments and anger, seemingly unable to move on. I sat and listened and tried to offer advice. After months of this pattern not shifting, I decided that, as a friend, I owed them a new and more honest approach. I said that when we next met up we would chat for fifteen minutes at the start of our conversation about the ex, and the pain and the revenge wanted, and then we would need to move on to something else. It might sound harsh but I felt it wasn't helpful to keep going round in circles and what might be needed was a shift in energy and conversation. This was actually met with total understanding and a sense of relief from my mate.

As I have mentioned, I am part of a blended family and, as much as I kind of hate that term as I just see us as a family, communication is key with so many of us in the mix. We have four kids all at different ages and all with different agendas. My husband and I both have weird jobs with little structure or certainty and he travels quite a bit. Without communication, our family would fall apart.

That's not to say that this constant communication is always pretty. My truth differs from Jesse's as we both have different natures and agendas yet we have to find a way to create harmony. My need for order and organisation isn't at the top of Jesse's list of priorities, while his living in the moment often gets on my nerves as I love to plan ahead. We both have good intentions but they look very different. We have to chat constantly about the kids and their wellbeing, their personal growth and what might be best for all of us. It can be tiring and might get in the way of fun but this sort of debate and sometimes heated conversation is so very needed. Luckily, this dynamic runs pretty well as we are both comfy speaking our truth with each other after nearly a decade of trial and error. I have learned to accept that it might not always be perfect but as long as we are talking and being honest, we'll work out a way.

DEAR GOOGLE AND JADA PINKETT SMITH

As I've been working on this book I've been thinking about why, so often, I will give others the power of opinion – trusting what they believe more than what I believe myself. Not only do I allow others' judgements of my truth to infiltrate my own ideas but I'll often ask other people for answers instead of trusting what I know. How many times have you thought, 'Am I doing life correctly?' I do all the time! I wonder if my work/social life ratio is 'right' or if the way I parent is 'right' or wonder if the fact that I like staying home a lot is 'wrong'. Why do I believe there is a right or wrong and why have I typed questions into search engines to find out the answers? 'Dear Google, is it normal to get in bed to read at 9:30 p.m. every night? Please say yes because I really enjoy it and don't want to stop.'

Or instead, I text a mate to ask them what they think I should do in life. Why am I feeling so insecure? Have you got the answer? Can you tell me it'll all be OK please so I don't have to figure it out myself? Maybe it's also because, if I let them give me the advice, I won't have to be so accountable for the outcome! I constantly give others the power and diminish my own truth to something weak and easily influenced. Of course, there is great value in discussing problems and ideas with friends and wise advice can be found online but I think at times we prioritise outside opinions over what we already know within.

Last year, I interviewed the formidable Jada Pinkett Smith who talked about how her greatest liberation is having emotional independence. She walked into the studio with a bright yellow plush coat on, sat down opposite me and oozed calm and confidence. I instantly wanted to be her friend. I'm sure everyone does. I was scared but ready. I had done my prep, I knew what I wanted to ask.

For the first five minutes, we sussed each other out. She was seeing how deep I might go; I was gauging which subjects might be off limits. Quickly we relaxed and got into the most phenomenal chat – one I'll never forget. I had not heard of emotional independence before. What was this mythical phrase she spoke of? Can I have it? And if so, HOW? Jada talked of how developing emotional independence means she can now navigate most situations in life without consulting a friend, her husband or the internet. She understands herself better than anyone else so has worked towards becoming free from the constant worry that someone else might have a better answer or solution than she does.

WOW! I want this! I want all of this. I am nowhere near this emotional utopia yet but it's a good reminder that we can give over the power to others in these moments or trust what we already know. And when we're looking for answers outside, we must remember they are more likely to be found inside. (And for me, my truth KNOWS that reading in bed is so much better than going out! Lockdown proved it!)

LOOK IN THE MIRROR

In this chapter so far, we've established that we are not responsible for another person's reaction to our own truth, silence is A-OK, healthy debate is encouraged to reach understanding and boundaries and we won't be ostracised from society because of it, so why am I still so scared of speaking up?

After giving this a lot of thought, I think it actually boils down to being scared of ourselves. The initial question at the start of this chapter was, 'What if people don't want to hear it?' But weirdly I think the answer transcends that worry altogether. Perhaps other people and their reactions mirror our own fears about ourselves. Maybe the real worry is that they'll confirm the fear we hold within. Are we are scared of our own truth?

In reality, we're unlikely to be rejected for our life choices and how we express them; if anything, people will admire us for being true to ourselves. So really, the fear is only of our own truth and what living it would do to our comfortable lives. As I stated in the last chapter, facing up to our own truth could require great change, a lot of energy and losing old habits and that is of course all scary stuff.

When I've felt I needed to leave a relationship or job, I have felt so worried about what everyone would say once I made the move. I didn't want to hear their questions or concerns because I knew they would mirror my own. I didn't want to be asked 'what now?' or 'what if?'; I wanted to just keep the blinkers on and jump.

Every time I have jumped ship from a job, 90 per cent of

people have said, 'OH GOD why? Why would you leave such a great job, you're making a mistake!' Some haven't liked my truth as it perhaps made them look at whether they were being true to themselves. It has freaked me out to hear their fears but only because they are my fears too. My truth has manifested as a slightly off-piste career journey at times and that confuses people, which in turn perturbs me, but again only because it mirrors some of my own fear.

When we change or make decisions it forces those around us to look at their own lives. So, many of the opinions chucked your way will be much more about the person giving the opinion than you. We all like certainty, so when someone throws a big old curveball, those around them react with shock. The human brain wants the familiar – we want order and for life to make sense in the way we have it mapped out in our heads.

If the Covid-19 pandemic taught us anything, it's that we will cope in times of uncertainty but it won't always be easy. I have found it very unnerving having no idea how life is going to play out when all this is over. Of course, none of us really knows what the future holds, pandemic or no pandemic, but if we think about that too much our heads will explode. To truly honour the fact that we have no idea where we are headed, or where those around us are headed, means we are vulnerable. We are delicate and could easily bruise like a soft peach. Being humbled by the enormity of a pandemic has made us connect with our inner peach. We have had to notice how fragile life is and how we cannot guarantee any particular outcome. It's unnerving but you may have discovered, as I have during this weird time, that it's actually the most amazing opportunity to learn stuff about yourself.

I've had to see how I react when I have little control over the general mess in our family home as the kids are here all day long. It's always been a huge fear of mine that if my house is in disarray then I will mentally fall apart. That has of course not happened. I have also worried that if there was a point where I couldn't leave the house for more than a few days I would become depressed. I have always assumed keeping on the move was the thing that allowed me to keep positive and motivated. At the point of writing, I haven't left the house in three weeks and I feel absolutely fine. The uncertain seems terrifying but more often than not we can 100 per cent cope. We learn on the job and we adapt. Our brain tells us it needs order and certainty but when we are willing to let go and open our eyes to the unknown we can really unearth our own inner strength and resilience.

WHY I HATE TRADITIONAL FUN

Sometimes we don't speak our truth as we feel embarrassed and like we might be the only weirdo who thinks a certain way. How wonderfully narcissistic! I feel like this all the time: 'Maybe I'm the only one in the world who has felt like this!' Highly unlikely. I've learned that when you get talking you see that you're never, ever alone.

I met up with rapper, spoken word artist, podcast legend and all-round brilliant chap Scroobius Pip last year and had a brilliantly frank chat about life. Another surprising and joyful theme in me speaking my truth at work is that others

want to speak their truth to me! We talked about social-
ising and how overwhelming the modern world can be. He
eloquently voiced how he isn't very good at and doesn't enjoy
fun. Oh. My. God. Pip just spoke MY truth to me without
me even knowing that is how I actually felt. My truth was
unlocked by someone else's truth.

I've never been good at fun and I've not much enjoyed what
is classically depicted as 'fun'. Dancing wildly in nightclubs,
necking warm wine at house parties, dancing on tables in
bars. I usually shudder at the thought. I spent most of my
twenties with a sprained ankle because I thought I should
be in clubs wearing impractical calf-shattering stilettos but
feeling so absurdly uncomfortable most of the time that I
blurred my vision with alcohol. Now, don't get me wrong, of
course I did end up having fun on quite a few of these nights
but I'm still not sure that nightclubs and suspiciously blue
cocktails are where fun is for the real me.

Pip was the first person I had heard talk about not liking
fun in this way. Before our conversation, I spent years
thinking I was the only person who didn't enjoy classic fun.
I spent so long worrying there was something wrong with
me and that I was faulty in some way because my idea of
fun was much more quiet than the wild and crazy cliché. I
was too scared to admit this to anyone in case they thought
I was a little odd, but ultimately I was less afraid of their
judgement than my own because I already feared I was an
oddball. Pip openly and contentedly going against the grain
seemed inspiring and actually very cool, which allowed me
to see that my love of a quieter life could be a cool quirk too
rather than a deep worry.

I think about this particular concern a lot as, in my thirties, I've really honoured my truth and have stayed at home reading books and drinking tea. There have of course been wickedly fun weddings where my step-daughter Lola and I have quite literally taken over the dance floor, and moments of madness on holiday with gin and sunburnt cheeks, but these stick out as lovely memories maybe because they are infrequent and so more special. Now nearing the end of my thirties, I sometimes worry that I should push myself from my comfort zone more and try to have more fun in the way of going out and partying.

I sometimes feel I don't have proper clarity on whether I'm honouring my truth or retreating from life. Where is the line? What are the definitions? I've come to the conclusion that, because I am mostly exhausted from my kids waking in the night needing a wee or feeling scared of a potential alien invasion, plus juggling the work I love doing, this worry can wait for now. I usually just allow myself to park the thought and stick to what I know my truth to be today.

Perhaps in the future, when I'm struggling to get my then teenage kids out of bed and have gotten used to Sunday lie-ins again, I'll have another dose of energy for what we deem to be classic fun. For now, I can't spread myself too thinly as I want to stay well and healthy. So I have decided to divide most of my time between our four kids and marriage and my work. That feels like my truth now, even if it doesn't align with what Instagram shows me fun looks like or what my mates are sometimes doing on a Saturday night. Maybe that classic idea of fun is in the future for me but it isn't today and that's all I can work with.

HONESTY BREEDS HONESTY

With the friends I have today, I can be pretty bloody honest. Not long before the pandemic, four of us tried to arrange a dinner on a WhatsApp group, among many conflicting work obligations and family timetables. I felt tired just thinking about it but love these mates dearly and wanted to see them.

'We're all thinking 7 p.m. for dinner right?' I pressed send with pursed lips, wondering if maybe it seemed bossy and perhaps a little tragic that I wanted dinner so early.

'6:30 p.m. would be even better for me' typed back one friend, adding a laughing emoji.

PHEW!

We're all exhausted, we all need our sleep and, by being honest about what I need in order to see my friends, I've helped out a friend who's feeling just the same. Our truths weren't so different.

It's the same with the bulkier, knottier, sensitive issues in life too. I talk very little about the catalyst behind my own depression because I'm still working on acceptance and understanding around that time of my life. I don't want to publicly talk about every detail because I know I'm not strong enough to deal with that being a wider conversation just yet. However, I have entrusted a few great mates with my feelings around the darker parts of my story. But I'm never, ever not shitting myself when revealing the depths of my depression and the parts I'm still making peace with.

On one occasion, under a blooming cherry blossom tree in a friend's back garden, I felt safe to talk. I opened up and laid out my darkest and trickiest fears and emotions.

I released them from the gloomiest crevices of my being and let my friend digest them, the risk being she could then judge me or see me as damaged, weak, not worthy of friendship. But instead a beautiful thing happened. She also reached inwards and heaved out her heaviness. She let her story unfurl with as many nerves jangling as I'd had about how my story might be received. She let her heart open and connect with mine in a way it hadn't before.

Honesty breeds honesty. If you let your truth out you'll usually see you're not alone as you imagine. It's a magical feeling.

GETTING FRIENDLY WITH FEAR

When we communicate our truth, the judgemental reactions of others can make us wobble so it is important to always root back to the decisions we have made and why.

If you feel judged for your decisions, try to remember that this reaction speaks volumes about the other party involved, much more so than it does about you. Your truth is who you are and this should not be diluted or changed to suit others. If the person you love doesn't fit someone else's truth; if the job you have chosen doesn't please someone else's truth; if the way you act, dress, express yourself doesn't complement someone else's truth, that is not your problem.

In these moments, we must remember and be open to viewing other people's fear. Every person who has a disapproving opinion about you and your truth is only really highlighting their own fear. Maybe it's worth looking at what they might be scared of. Are they worried because they know they are not living an honest and truthful life? Are they terrified of how your life changes might affect them and their truth? Are they angry because they don't feel courageous enough to live their truth? Recognising other people's fears will allow us to have empathy and compassion so we can continue to live truthfully and help others to follow suit.

The conclusion I have come to over the years is that we fear other people's opinions because they are the fears we already hold about ourselves. And the fears of others are only triggered because they see your powerful truth mirroring back at them something that they have their own issues with. For instance, I would never worry that someone might think I'm too quiet because that isn't a worry I already have about myself. I'm fine with being quiet, and don't mind anyone commenting on that. But if someone said I was annoying or selfish – that would trigger all of my worst fears about myself.

Other people's triggering opinions are not new thoughts or epiphanies to us, they are pre-existing fears. Fear is the number one condition holding us all back from simply being us. So, the first step in freeing ourselves from judgement is to get friendly with that fear. Never forget that those judging are only worried about how your truth makes them feel. Keep in mind that you're never alone; others will have spoken a truth similar to yours before. Speaking your truth won't lead to you being alone. Feel the fear and go for it!

MY FEARS THAT I DON'T WANT OTHERS TO RECOGNISE

★ That I am not good enough

★ That I don't push myself enough

★ That I am not smart

★ That my body looks wrong

★ That I haven't tried enough

★ That I am unkind

★ That I haven't helped enough

★ That I am unthoughtful

★ That I am undeserving of my opportunities

Write your list here
Get it off your chest.

_____

_____

_____

_____

_____

_____

_____

_____

_____

_____

_____

_____

_____

_____

_____

_____

_____

_____

_____

_____

_____

6

HOW CAN SPEAKING MY TRUTH ENHANCE MY LIFE?

Speaking up is probably always going to be scary. Let's get that straight. Being truthful – with yourself and others – is liberating and freeing but not always comfortable. Facing the truth often means facing the unknown, so with that comes vulnerability. Without our usual comforting beliefs and certainties, we feel as if our armour is off and all of our sensitive and soft bits are outside of our bodies: our heart open with blood pumping and vessels exposed; our life-supporting lungs expanding and pushing our proud chest forward to keep us safe; our eyes uncovered and blinking tears to show our true self.

Yet, I'm not sure about you, but most of the scary things I have been through have been the most groundbreaking in terms of making me a stronger, better, happier person. Those times have not necessarily been easy but they were certainly beneficial in the long run. Of course, we all want the safe option. We want for life to be comfortable and relaxing, but that comfort is often a lazy swap for the real and true. Maybe our first step in understanding the benefits of speaking our truth has to be accepting the scary moments and learning to perhaps even enjoy the fear.

WORRY, PINK CHEEKS AND RELIEF

In my darkest moments, speaking my truth has been out of the question. I have felt that there would be no benefit at all. Why would I want to compound what I'm going through by talking about it? It seemed preferable to pretend on the surface that everything was OK.

In these moments, the dam stopping the words from flowing is made entirely of shame. The mere thought of laying bare tricky feelings and emotions to others would make me feel drained, as shame highlights every fear going. Shame stops true connection as it wants you to be alone in your worry and sickness. Shame shouts that you will be judged, ostracised and labelled bad if you speak up. Some of us will carry shame around with us for years and often unknowingly. A healer I spoke with recently helped me unload shame I had been carrying around about certain thoughts and feelings since childhood. I hadn't even known it was there. The shame wasn't attached to any trauma or a big moment in my life yet it was still there rumbling along by my side for decades.

Often we assume everyone else will judge us for our

mistakes or worries so we use shame as a suit of armour to protect us. All it really does is slow down our rate of recovery from tough situations as shame stops us from talking about the parts of life that hurt. It shuts us down and closes us off from other people.

Good friends are brilliant at detecting pain and confusion even when we're wearing a mask of happiness on the outside. Their sniffer-dog noses sense the need for chat and rumination. On one occasion when I felt very alone and very confused, a good friend started up a conversation. She did what all skilled mates do and started by telling me her latest worries and concerns. Instantly feeling empathetic and wanting to match her honesty, I spilled out my heart. My fingers twitched nervously inside the sleeve of my jumper and my heart notched up to a sprinting beat; my cheeks stole all the colour, leaving my body grey but my face bright pink. I didn't want what I was saying to be real. I didn't want my truth to be heard but it came crashing out anyway. Of course, my story was met with understanding and a gentle touch of the arm, then I felt an immense sense of relief. Neck muscles loosened, I let out a large breath, eyes softened and tears flowed. That is connection. Acknowledging our truth and speaking it out loud might feel scary but I promise you the relief is worth it.

Yet, on a lighter note, with less critical or serious issues there can still be such a release of mental and physical tension. I remember a dynamic at work many years ago that I found tricky. So many tiny things about the way my colleague worked riled me and saw my neck tendons rising towards my ears. I let it brew, I let it simmer. Silly things that were insignificant in the grand scheme of my life had the potency to boil my day to heat and bubbles. Why didn't I speak up? Why didn't I ask if we could work in a different way or if he could try changing a few minor ways in which he worked so that he could understand me better and I could work with him in the best possible way? I think I'm always waiting for something bad to happen, a punishment for having my say and asking another to make changes. A fear that my opinion might be wrong or too bold and therefore I'll be damned down the line. A nonsensical and quite religious fear considering I don't align to one particular faith. So instead I kept silent and felt terrible. There was even a moment where we went for coffee to iron a few things out and I still couldn't find the courage to politely mention what I needed in order for me to work to my best ability. If I had spoken up I'm sure we could have found new methods to cohesively work together, but it never got that far. The particular team I was working with naturally dispersed but I felt like I had behaved badly and that I'd let myself down by not speaking up. Speaking up in these smaller moments might feel awkward and like little Bunsen burners are at the ready in your cheeks, but the freedom and lack of stress is so, so worth it.

WELCOME BACK BODY, YOU'RE MINE

Growing up, I thought little about my physical silhouette. I was way too busy climbing trees and wearing Hyper-color T-shirts to pay attention to the fact that I had broad shoulders or larger than average nostrils or a tiny pot belly.

My body was just there, it wasn't something I needed to think about. My truth was, and of course still is, that I have a beautiful, healthy body that works miracles and allows me so much freedom. I took that for granted as a child whereas now it is something I have had to work for, and I remind myself to be grateful for my body in daily affirmations. I take time throughout the day to praise the wonder of my very own human body.

And yet there was a huge chunk of time, between my childhood and now, when I had a very different relationship with my body. I allowed my truth and understanding of my own physicality to be questioned and challenged by magazines, clothing companies and the shine of the world of showbiz. Possibly this was amplified for me as a teenager due to how much exposure I had to the entertainment industry, where appearance is everything, yet maybe not. How many of us have had our opinions of ourselves and our bodies influenced by how women are talked about in the media? How many have felt their body confidence ravaged by the images we see every day? Way too many to count.

Like most of us, I can't pinpoint an exact date or time when I went from being unquestionably content in my body to wishing it was different. But I can look back at the damage done over the years and piece together why I lost my truth. Fluorescent bubble letters luring me into the glamour and perfection of life depicted in magazines with button-nosed girls wearing tiny-waisted jean shorts. Then music videos featuring nineties crop tops and flat, shimmering stomachs. Tights, leotards and the most beautifully performed split leap at my local dance school. Could it have been one of them? Or all of them, cascading from the top of the consumer food chain.

It's too easy to believe we need to fit into small clothes and diminish ourselves, physically and emotionally, as for so long the narrative has been that women have to look a certain way to be desired. The more insecure we are, the easier it is to offer us solutions to buy – diets, clothes, make-up. I didn't understand any of this broader context growing up; instead, like so many of us, I started to see my own body as faulty. Only in tiny increments at first. A pair of corduroy flares that wouldn't zip up on *The Disney Club* TV show, then regular exposure to minuscule real-life popstars sat next to me on an inflatable sofa. This was followed by the surreal visual of seeing my own image staring at me from inside a magazine, inviting me to pick apart flesh and form, making my own body the enemy.

This gradual warping of my own truth about my body was the beginning of years of physical abuse. The bulimia started around nineteen years of age. There had always been a comfort in eating for me and a slightly all-or-nothing attitude to life, so when I found myself in work environments with free food flowing and a TV company footing the bill, I was unstoppable. Instead of seeing this for what it was – a coping mechanism in a situation where I was uncomfortable – I beat myself up for what I saw as shameful greed.

Then, on one occasion, an idea entered my head out of nowhere. I would get rid of the guilt and shame of not being as disciplined as those around me by throwing up what I'd eaten. I wanted to be like the shinier TV people who seemed to be coping just fine with their jobs and able to resist free buffets. Bulimia was a new secret equation that allowed me to flush away my sins and have control over a part of my life, as the rest of it felt overwhelming. I still had a wonderful, grounded and encouraging family and gang of school friends, but my new, complex job opened up a lot of internal chaos that I didn't know how to deal with. My little secret went on for years but usually without actual binges. All it would take was one mouthful too many or choosing a sweet treat over the nutritious option and that was enough of a trigger to have me disappear from a room to facilitate my want for release.

Ten years of physical self-punishment has left me with sadness, regret and gum damage on one side of my mouth but I'm lucky I have reconnected with my truth. As incrementally as the external lies set in about my body, so they gradually started to mean a lot less to me. Then, like many women, my relationship with my body changed as soon as I got pregnant. The desire to look like Kate Moss in jeans was dwarfed by the all-encompassing want for a healthy, bouncing baby.

During my first pregnancy I ate cheese in handfuls, feeling nothing but pleasure. No guilt in sight. I sent Jesse out late-night taco hunting on the mean streets of west London to satisfy my cravings. Again, no guilt, just comfort and total pleasure. Post-birth and a little way down the line, as mum to blue-eyed Rex Rayne Wood, I felt the familiar guilt of eating creep back in but I managed to keep my brain on track, understanding that I needed to be healthy and strong for my family. I know I should be making good choices for myself but I find it much easier to bear in mind my responsibilities for those I love.

Today, I know my truth about my body – and it is that it can do wonderful things. I may still feel tense around food or changes in my diet and occasionally slip into loathing my body but the truth is my body is wonderful. Just reminding myself of that means I haven't slipped back into bad habits. I know my body is miraculous so my truth tells me I have to honour it daily. My brain may try to trick me into believing otherwise but not enough for me to physically punish it anymore.

I don't want to make this progress sound easy, as it hasn't been, and nor did it happen overnight. I do advise that if you are struggling with issues around eating and body image it might be useful to seek professional help or get in touch with one of the many brilliant charities that offer assistance and advice. Mind and Beat are two excellent charities that understand the complexities and intricacies of having an eating disorder.

Today I feel grateful that I can get up in the morning and run. My body allows me to do that. How could I punish myself after that? I will celebrate my muscly legs and the distance they travelled. I can bend and flex and let yoga flow through me. I grew babies in my uterus and pushed them out, with each magical part of my body knowing what to do. I can sit here today and look at my body with its broad shoulders, characterful nose, squishy tummy from pregnancy, weakened pelvic floor from labour, bitten finger-nails, small boobs and skinny ankles and feel nothing but gratitude. On bad days, I might forget the truth and feel negatively towards my own flesh but I can bring myself back to it because I've taken it back as mine. My body, my truth.

Knowing my truth in this case has given me a freedom I denied myself for years. Welcome back body, you're mine.

LOOK AT YOUR BODY

It's all too easy to be distracted from our own truth by the 'perfect' images of other bodies that we see around us, from social media to films, television and magazines. We need to be aware of this distraction every time we feel our sense of truth wilt as we compare ourselves to the perfection (often filtered) that we see elsewhere. First of all, though, we must remember that there is no magic equation: looking amazing does not mean feeling amazing. The supposedly perfect-looking body doesn't mean the perfect life.

The potential for endless comparison between ourselves and what we see around us is perhaps even more of a problem today than it was when I was growing up, as there are so many more images available to us on Instagram and other platforms. But rather than feeling insecure, we can choose to follow those accounts that highlight how wonderful our bodies are, just for existing. Those mavericks who give us other options and the chance to celebrate our bodies without guilt or shame. If you want to follow people who make you feel good, first think of all of the things that genuinely make you tick. Don't just hunt out accounts full of pretty pictures and perfection.

I love art so adore following Jonathan Yeo and Noel Fielding. I love honesty so choose to follow people like Busy Philipps and Bryony Gordon. I love gushing over nature so follow Earth Focus and the WWF. If it's body confidence you're looking for on social media get following my friend Poorna Bell who is beyond articulate and wonderful, and also Annie Price, who has faced many hurdles in life but remains one of my go-to people for a boost. These people inspire me and make me remember my good bits, physical or not.

The truth for all of us is that our bodies are bloody marvellous and work miracles every day without us even thinking about it. Our hair is just quietly growing away while we do the dishes; our lungs are inflating and releasing, keeping us oxygenated and alive while we watch TV; our heart is cleverly pumping our blood around our bodies while we sleep at night. We are perfect as we are. We knew this as tiny kids and we have to remember it now. We do not need to change and should not feel guilt or shame around our physical bodies. The benefit of remembering this truth is freedom! It might take work, daily affirmations, speaking to oneself in the mirror in a positive way or taking inspiration from body-positive people but, once you get there, as I slowly am, you will feel liberated. And that is only going to clarify and intensify the relationship you have with your own body. Loving your body as it is means more energy, a freedom in movement when out in public, the courage to dress how you really want, better sex and less self-loathing all round.

REGRET AND SAYING SORRY

I also believe that speaking our truth helps us to lessen feelings of regret. I am not one of those people who has no regret. I understand the notion of 'Oh well, I wouldn't be here today if that terrible thing hadn't happened', but also I would very much like that terrible thing to have NOT happened.

I think some of the time regret comes from feeling unsure where to turn. We want to do something so badly but get stuck with fear, soldered to the spot, unable to put one foot forward. For instance, if your parents or those who care for you in life have made it clear that academic success is all that matters, how do you reconcile that with your own longing for creativity and flexibility? This particular crossroad has been faced by millions of people over the years and it hasn't been easy for any of them. Yet I'm sure the ones who took the road that led to their truth ended up a lot happier with less regret. I'm not ignoring the huge family upheaval that might come with challenging a loved one's hopes or expectations, but I do think that taking positive steps towards our truth gives us so much opportunity and a lust for life. As we have seen, the opinions of others really have little to do with finding and living our truth.

When regret comes from things we've done then we have to find acceptance and forgiveness. If you know there are moments you regret, can you own up to them? Along with most people, I've said my share of stupid things, treated people badly, ignored people I found tricky. Speaking our truth around these moments allows us to recognise them, rather than pretending they didn't happen, only for them to bite you on the arse down the line. Maybe admitting a transgression or mistake to yourself means you feel you have to apologise. This can be awkward and tough but ultimately freeing.

Every time I apologise to Jesse for my bad behaviour, I dread it beforehand but feel so free afterwards. It is like a release. Saying sorry is HARD but it's one of the best ways to remember, and reconnect with, our truth. It opens up our sense of responsibility and gives us control over a situation that feels uncomfortable. Our kids are so used to watching us apologise to each other after a shitty row or bad, overtired behaviour that they are now both natural apologisers. Rex is prone to a forty-five-minute tantrum which you think he may never return from, yet, somewhere down the line, he'll slope over with his shoulders hunched and say, 'Sorry, Mummy.' I'm not a perfect parent but I'm proud of that one.

When reading Russell Brand's book, *Recovery*, about overcoming addiction and the twelve-step initiative, I found the chapter and step about apology so compelling. This advises apologising to all those to whom you have caused harm over the years, unless doing so may cause more harm. Wow, to me that revelation felt cinematic. I could almost sense the relief from this momentous challenge. Tough and beautiful in equal measure.

I recently reached out to someone who I haven't spoken to in years because, although it wasn't a daily worry, I did have an underlying heaviness due to the unfinished nature of our friendship. I was nervous and expected no response but it led to a lovely conversation and definitely a little more peace. There are still some out there who I need to apologise to and maybe if I bump into them I will feel strong enough to speak up and say sorry, thereby offering both myself and the other person some peace.

Is there anyone in your life who needs an apology from you? Can you find a way to let them know you're sorry?

LET'S TALK ABOUT SEX

Talking openly about sex is just not something we do very often I guess, at least not without averted eyes and red cheeks. We rarely bring up the subject at dinner with our mates or discuss our worries about it in a family situation. There is still a slightly Victorian prudishness in place that stops us from speaking our truth around it. As a culture, we are somewhat repressed when it comes to sex, but hiding this important truth about ourselves can create shame, concern and isolation.

I recently chatted to Flo Perry on my podcast about her book, *How to Have Feminist Sex*. It wasn't until I read Flo's work that I realised I had been slightly dodging the subject too. Although we'd recorded more than sixty Happy Place podcasts at that point, this was the first episode where we even touched on sex. As Flo says, sex is complicated. It's possibly the most intimate form of communication humans have and it can get messy if not talked about properly and thoroughly. Now, I'm sure, like me, some of you might not have spoken up when you're either uncomfortable or not happy with how sex is playing out. Especially when you're younger, the thought of saying how you really feel in a sexual relationship seems to be a complete no-go.

We're mainly scared of rejection so just go along with what seems to be the norm – but if we don't talk about it, how do we really know what the norm is? Busy Philipps, the American actor, recently said on an episode of Happy Place that as a youngster she believed 'sex just happened to girls'. What an interesting and observant look at how so many young people feel! We grow up fascinated by sex but not fully able to grasp how we can have control and agency over it. It's so important that we learn to cut through the awkwardness and believe we are allowed to truthfully express our wants and desires, as well as articulating what we don't feel comfortable with.

There are of course varying types of communication when it comes to sex. Let's start with the more common sexual stutters that we've probably all experienced. If you're not speaking your truth to your partner can you look at why? Is there a relationship imbalance between you? Do you feel like your partner takes the lead in life so you've allowed them to do the same in your sex life too? Or do you get the say too often yet don't ask how your partner feels?

I'm pretty sure that so many words get pushed down into the depths of our being around sex because we feel embarrassed and awkward and fear rejection. Flo Perry suggests that to find your truth in your sex life you need to be in touch with your own fantasies first. Learn what really turns you on and helps you to get out of your head and more into your body and switch off those insecurities. Only you know what works for you. Flo recommended making this a fun and sexy conversation that also allows you to speak honestly, rather than something to dread or feel awkward about. The benefit here, of course, is a renewed autonomy over your sexual encounters rather than putting up with them or just going through the motions for the sake of someone else's pleasure. We all have the right to speak our truth around our own desires and needs. Sex should, of course, be fun, relaxing and something that helps us feel connected. Like speaking any truth out loud, it might not be a comfortable thought to start up this line of conversation but it could have a very positive outcome.

In the face of past trauma or post-traumatic stress disorder around sex, this kind of honesty becomes much trickier and I'm sure for those who have endured it, speaking up can feel almost impossible. So many people today suffer the heartbreaking and confusing consequences of sexual assault. Having not been through this myself, I can't offer any solid advice, but would always assume that talking to other people who have experienced similar trauma or to a professional would be helpful.

Talk therapy is always a good way of speaking your truth as you are in a safe space and will be supported by an experienced person while you gather confidence. Finding groups where you can speak your truth is another great way to help diminish negative feelings around the past and to forge genuine connection and understanding from others. To speak your truth after experiencing such trauma is one of the bravest things you can do.

As part of the #MeToo movement, we saw so many courageous people stand up to speak their truth on the matter very publicly. This movement has created some visible change, which again demonstrates the power and benefit of speaking your truth. From adversity, you can spark positive change which benefits not just yourself, but others. It's not an easy thing to do but it can be profoundly powerful.

SEXUALITY, GENDER AND COMMUNITY

Sexuality and gender are complex and, thankfully, due to increased conversation around these topics in recent years, they are something that we now understand to be infinitely varied. Although we may have a wider understanding of sexuality and gender, and their fluidity, there are still unfortunately often social boundaries in place that hinder us from having further open and much-needed discussions about them.

In the last hundred years, we have seen individuals overcome their own comfort levels to talk openly about their sexuality and gender, and that has led to great change in how people might decide to talk about their experience. Billie Jean King, Stephen Fry, Jonathan Van Ness, Ellen DeGeneres, Juno Dawson among many others have opened up the conversation and created support for the LGBTQ+ community, but there is still a lack of understanding from some around sexuality and indeed gender. Still today, far too many people fear their own sexuality and gender so they remain repressed and unhappy. It's a tricky subject for me to talk about as a straight married woman so if you are in need of help in dealing with your own sexuality or gender, I always prefer to point to people doing incredible work in this area. Their advice and guidance is to be listened to and honoured. They're the ones on the front line of personal discomfort and at times discrimination. They're the ones making a change. Follow, or search for those who are leading the way in this conversation – particularly my dear friend Gok Wan, the aforementioned Jonathan Van Ness, Ellen Page, Keegan Hirst and the Instagram account Queerbible – if you feel you have yet to speak your truth around your own sexuality or gender.

What I do feel comfortable saying is that those I know who have told their own story talk about a huge sense of relief as they live their truth and grow stronger as a result. And they no longer feel the shame of hiding a secret. It has, for all, been terrifying at times, draining in moments and frustrating that they've had to explain themselves or fend off ignorant questions and comments.

My friend Gok Wan has faced all sorts of idiotic abuse from strangers on social media, and occasionally in public, purely due to his sexuality. Sloppy words hurled his way for no other reason than the instigator is full of fear and ignorance in their own life. It has never deterred Gok from living his truth and from talking about it to help others. I was in awe when Jonathan Van Ness from *Queer Eye* openly talked about being HIV positive. His willingness to speak his truth allowed many others to open up about their own stories, get proper help and also eradicate unnecessary shame and worry. His work has had a profound effect on so many people – both those who are coming to terms with a diagnosis and those ignorant enough to judge without understanding. Proper angel work!

No one should live life feeling shame. Speaking our truth allows us to eliminate this huge hidden burden and lighten our lives. Culturally, shame only exists because of the ignorance of a small minority. These negative opinions usually gain traction because fear snowballs and people who are already scared grab hold of more things to worry about and therefore ignore and condemn others. If we talk, tell our stories and connect with others these heavy emotions can dissipate and make way for big, bold understanding and love, thwacking fear to one side so that new avenues can be paved.

Understanding your own truth can of course be devastating if your family have specific religious beliefs about sexuality and gender. Or if you've made decisions that could potentially mean losing someone you love from your life who can't accept your truth. But shouldn't we all be allowed to experience our truth? The liberation of telling the world who we are? I think so, and will always support those who make the choice to live life in the way they want to. It takes a lot of courage to talk about sexuality and gender, in whatever form it takes, but ultimately speaking out offers us the freedom we all deserve.

CREATE BOUNDARIES NOT WALLS

As well as liberation, a physical lack of tension and the chance to create community, speaking our truth also gives us the confidence to create boundaries. Without boundaries relationships fray and confusion is caused. As I mentioned earlier, when I was younger I was an expert in *not* setting boundaries. My fear of outside judgement stopped me in my tracks and squashed the words back down that would have expressed how I felt. Many of my friendships have broken down because of it; many arguments have exploded and much resentment has gathered. I have been so worried others will think I'm creating a wall rather than a reasonable boundary.

I remember clearly every school year sitting at my desk in my new pair of Kickers, fringe blow-dried and lip liner strong, really fearing my new form tutor. You may remember from your own childhood that the first week, or even month of term is when the new teacher is the toughest. At times they can seem almost unfriendly. You don't like this teacher at first and feel like there are too many rules and not enough smiles. You don't understand their new ways or why they have to bark orders in an army major way. But halfway through the school year, you've grown to love them. Looking back as an adult, you understand their need for order – they were establishing boundaries, without which it would have been *Lord of the Flies*. With strong boundaries respect is gained and everyone knows where they stand. They help the teacher create a dynamic that works for you to learn and for them to teach. It's no different in our everyday lives.

When we meet a new person or initiate a new relationship, we have to establish boundaries so everyone knows their part in the dynamic. Boundaries for children are safety and comfort even when they seem to hate it, and it's no different for adults.

Boundaries in adult relationships mean we are able to state our needs clearly and to allow others to do the same.

Easier said than done, of course. I find it almost excruciating to ask for a thing. I'm the person who wants to make everyone tea with their preferred milk/sugar/teabag option, wash up all the mugs afterwards and will still feel I haven't done enough. I have so often subconsciously felt that if I spoke up and asked for something to be done differently or for that person to give me their time and energy then maybe they would dislike me or think I was taking the piss.

I'm much better at this today as I work in a big team at Happy Place and need for everyone to feel part of it and like they're bringing something to the table – but previously I have been scared to say my bit and speak my truth. Shit-scared, to be honest. I have chosen exhaustion and feeling overstretched rather than asking someone to lighten my load. I have been run-down and moody rather than opting to have someone do something for me. And I have let that turn into resentment as I haven't spoken up until way too far down the line. It's been one of the lessons I've had to learn again and again but I'm now seeing the benefits.

With honesty and clear boundaries, I have much healthier work and personal relationships today. In those moments where I still feel awkward and fear rejection, I remind myself that creating boundaries allows a relationship to last and be strong enough to sustain the unexpected.

HELLO ME

Another benefit of speaking the truth that I've recently discovered is that we can get much more in touch with how we feel about OURSELVES. We often don't actually know ourselves very well at all. Behaviour becomes second nature and we forget to distinguish between what is habitual and what is true.

Not long before lockdown, I was sent a triggering email. Nothing serious at all, but it flustered me. Once I stepped away from the screen to consider the words with a little detachment, I could see that my reaction was more about how I think about MYSELF rather than how I felt about the email and the person who sent it. The email was a reply to one of mine in which I had explained how I wouldn't be able to do something during one part of the summer as I would be on a family holiday in Ibiza for a couple of weeks (although at the point of writing, it seems highly unlikely any of us will be travelling anytime soon. A staycation in Costa del SW London will do us just fine). The reply from the other person seemed to have raised eyebrows and a 'lucky for some' tone around it.

Anger. Neck tension. Blood-curdling rage. My initial monologue set to, 'I work bloody hard all year round, I want to treat my family to time in the sun. I've worked since I was fifteen to afford summer holidays.' It was a self-right-eous and frankly slightly vindictive mental response from me. Now, I know deep down I'm very lucky to be able to go on holiday and I know that it's not necessarily normal for everyone. Being able to take two weeks abroad is not something I take for granted. So why did I find this email so triggering? Because the truth, MY truth, is that, deep down, I don't believe I deserve it either. The eyebrow-raising tone to the email mirrored my own lack of belief that I should be going. The red-hot rage surged through me because the person who sent the email was speaking MY truth.

How funny that these moments of anger can unearth how we really feel about ourselves. If we want to then align with our truth and fix these moments of energy wasted on anger we have two choices. In that moment, I could either surrender to the knowledge that I have trouble believing I deserve good stuff or I could work with a positive affirmation to try to combat this old, habitual way of thinking. I find affirmations so, so helpful as they are a practical action and can help to redirect my thoughts even when I'm still struggling to believe what I'm saying. So once I had identified my trigger, I repeatedly told myself, out loud, 'I am deserving of lovely times. I am deserving of lovely experiences.'

The truth is that ALL of us are deserving of lovely experiences, whatever that means for each of us.

I can now only thank the possibly jealous emailer for provoking some self-inventory which acted as a catalyst for some much-needed personal change. Sometimes our perceived truth needs challenging. What I mean here is that there is our truth – which is our knowing and our absolute full-bodied, gut-warming, soul-grounding understanding of love and connection – and then there is the *perceived* truth, which is the lies we've believed or told ourselves. So, in this instance my perceived knowledge was that I am not deserving. It's not true but I've believed it long enough for it to feel real. My perceived truth needed challenging to reach my real truth, which is that I am deserving, I am enough and I am good. Use tricky situations to reveal your perceived truth and let that help you explore your own habits and mental thought patterns to uncover the real truth!

After writing this chapter, I'm not sure I see many disadvantages of speaking one's truth. Maybe the only one being it is often hard in the moment. Fragile moments where we feel vulnerable and scared usually always lead to benefits. The ways in which speaking your truth can enhance your life are a sense of freedom, liberation, healthy relationships, agency over our lives and the chance to help others.

What does freedom look like to you?

_____

_____

_____

_____

_____

_____

_____

_____

_____

_____

_____

What do boundaries look like to you?

_____

_____

_____

_____

_____

_____

_____

_____

_____

_____

_____

_____

_____

_____

_____

Ten things you love about your body:

1. _____

2. _____

3. _____

4. _____

5. _____

6. _____

7. _____

8. _____

9. _____

10. _____

7

CAN I HELP OTHERS SPEAK THEIR TRUTH?

Helping others speak their truth is complex. It requires empathy, compassion and perhaps a little patience – three very underrated and much-needed qualities. It's common to long for beauty, charisma and bedazzling warmth but less common to cultivate the qualities we need to keep relationships rock-solid and our sanity intact.

There are reasons why those around us might not be speaking their truth. Sometimes this might affect us greatly as we love and care for these individuals, and sometimes it may just trigger us to look at ourselves a little more closely. Both examples are worth a good snoop around.

One lesson I have learned again and again is to always reach out to another if you see or believe they are struggling with their truth. Although the conversation around mental health is widening there is still a lot of shame associated with it in certain communities, workplaces and families. Reaching out to another will always give that person another layer of support and comfort. They may not choose to share their truth with you immediately but knowing that they can is a support in itself.

Recently one of my good friends was in the middle of a painful breakup. We text daily and I could feel the pain seeping through the screen on my phone. As an outsider, it is always much easier to have a greater perspective on a matter as the truth isn't clouded by tricky emotions. The breakup was dragging on as, although my friend was unhappy and had been treated badly, they were still finding it very hard to let go. Having been in the same situation many years ago, I was able to recall that pain, but I could also remember the freedom I felt after the final cord had been cut. I sent daily texts reminding my friend that they deserved the best. This was the absolute truth. They didn't deserve to put up with any more emotional abuse or turmoil and needed a clean break. I initiated conversations about whether they truly believed they were deserving of love, which started up a healthy open dialogue about how tough we all are on ourselves. I have hopefully helped this dear friend see their own truth: that a clean break is needed for some time out and clarity and that they truly deserve wonderful things.

WHEN THE PAIN SPILLS OUT

Often, we can make informed guesses about how our loved ones feel without any words being spoken. We know when someone we are close to doesn't quite feel right. The discomfort clings to the air around them, it inhabits the silence in between words and creates new creases on their forehead. We know, we can see it, but sometimes we still do nothing.

While I have reached out to some in need, I also have huge regret about not asking certain people in my life if they needed help. I've either presumed they've already got enough support or subconsciously thought I had nothing to offer. Usually help is welcomed with open arms. Occasionally our offer will be rejected and, in those moments, we must ask ourselves whether help is genuinely not needed or perhaps needed even more than we first thought. Some people don't want to be any trouble and feel they must struggle alone.

I believe when someone is struggling it is quite often because they are not speaking their truth. They are denying a part of themselves and it starts to show. Behaviour changes, tensions build and then it all starts to spill out. The body can't hold it any longer. When someone in your life isn't speaking their truth, they may be passive-aggressive as they can't contain the frustration. They might be extra-quiet as the words seem impossible to form. They might use something to cover the truth: alcohol, shopping, drugs, food, obsessive cleaning, sleeping too much, or any other habitual behaviour that stops us looking at the truth.

I know when I am trying to avoid the truth I'll keep myself very busy indeed. My chosen tactic is usually cleaning. I think there must be something subconscious going on; maybe I believe I can clean away the worry or the thought that's niggling me. I'll clean out whole cupboards, rearrange sock drawers, scrub the floors until they shine. I now know that when I start cleaning like this, I'm usually trying to work through anger which is one of my go-to emotions when something isn't sitting right. I'll push every bit of red-hot rage into the scrubbing brush, I'll vanquish all frustration with a vigorous swipe of my cloth to shelf. My house might look immaculate afterwards but I'm still left with the truth: I'm pissed off about something and I need to sort it out. I need to dive beneath the anger that resides on the surface and see what is really going on.

We can often recognise the habitual behaviour of our loved ones when they are going through something too. We know that certain traits might mean they are trying to numb the truth. For one person their numbing sounds like a bottle of sparkling wine popping and fizzing open followed by a few vodkas every night. Or it might look like a late-night bowl of cereal and several sandwiches to fill a hole. Numbing can also take the form of a full shopping basket on a retail website. Behaviour speaks, and we can pick up on it if we are tuned in to that person. Pay attention to your own triggers, and to the triggers of those you love, to identify what is really going on. What truth is being numbed?

THE NEED FOR SILENCE

Our eyes are often one of the biggest giveaways to how we truly feel. Eyes that sparkle and are open wide with wonder speak the truth. Unafraid eyes welcome every experience and emotion. Closed, dull eyes that avoid another's gaze are hiding eyes. Eyes that want to speak and tell their story but really don't know where to start. I can recognise this most easily in my kids. I can look into their little eyes and instantly sense if they're struggling. Rex's eyes look grey rather than blue when he is working through something. Honey's look tired and narrower when she is processing something. This is when I know I can step in and try to help them work out what their truth is.

Reaching out to someone in your life who may need support or help isn't easy. Any sort of intervention or outstretched hand for support might be met with defensiveness or even a push away. Before you feel offended, it's imperative to remember the moments where you have felt similarly closed off from the world and rejected help. We must recall how that fear felt so we can work out the best way to approach difficult subjects and support from the heart and not the head.

If we are able to step into that person's life and properly offer support to help them reveal their truth then we need to make sure our ears are ready. We need to ask ourselves whether we are truly listening or just picking out the bits of their story that apply to our own. It is so easy to make someone else's story a portal for your own pain and history. I'm sure we've all done it in the past. Thinking we're being helpful, we've found an opportunity to be nostalgic for a few moments, waxing lyrical about our own pain and suffering, thinking it might lighten the other person's load.

I'm susceptible to this one as I often get nervous in these uncomfortable moments and want to fill the gaps. When I know someone is being very real with me and they feel comfortable enough to show me their heart and pain I so desperately don't want to get my bit wrong. I want to be supportive and help them if I can. I have previously filled silent pauses with agreement and personal stories when, really, we both just needed silence.

Weirdly, my podcast Happy Place has helped me get over this as I'm often privileged enough to be in the presence of someone who is willing to go there. I have sat and listened to courageous individuals tell their story and have felt compelled to just let them control the conversation without my non-stop verbal validation. I've learned it is much more powerful to sit still, quietly, and properly listen. Listening doesn't always require action. Sometimes the action is in the quiet bits. It's the unspoken current of understanding in the warmth of a gaze, an attentive posture and the sharing of positive energy. This gives the other person space to speak their truth without being interrupted.

Through recording Happy Place, I have learned that if I leave a little silence after the other person has stopped talking then they usually carry on to say something they were at first hesitant to articulate. You offer a little more space and they fill it with what's really going on. If we are too quick to agree, to fill a silence or come up with our own theory then we rob the other person of space to explore how they really feel. I am a talkative person so I sometimes assume everybody else is, but what I've realised from doing the podcast is that some people don't talk about their emotions much. If you give them permission to do so with carefully laid, tender silence then they feel much more inclined to explore emotion for themselves. In those pockets of silence often lies the truth.

HEAR ME NOW

Some of us get to the point of not bothering to speak up because we don't believe we'll be heard anyway. I have felt like this, and I'm sure you have too. The people in your life who are suffering most likely feel this way and need space to be heard and seen. So just be ears. Let your heart open to them without judgement, keep your ears soft and still and just simply listen. It's often enough.

With this active listening often comes a huge personal relief. Last year a friend and I decided to tell each other one thing about ourselves we felt ashamed of. A single incident each that had warped our own truth. We both had a story powerful enough to wake us shuddering from the most slumber-drenched sleep. A tale that makes cheeks redden and muscles clench as you try to will it away. God, it was not easy to say it out loud. Each word from my mouth came out slowly and sluggishly as if it might retreat for eternity. My eyes looked at the carpet and my twitching feet. My knees knocked like branches in the wind. My heart pounded, awaiting judgement and the ever-feared rejection. My friend sat and listened. She didn't speak. She then told her story with as much internal horror and fear. She coughed and paused and stumbled through a small story from her past which felt uncertain and soul-baring. I sat. I listened. I did not speak.

When we had finished telling our stories, we both laughed. Properly laughed. There was no more fear. We had spoken our shame out loud and we were not rejected or judged. We were able to rewrite our truth and lose a lot of self-loathing in the process. These stories were not as soul-baring as we had imagined because they weren't connected to the soul at all. They felt exposing, sure, but these old, stuck stories weren't our truth. They were small human mistakes that we had learned from. They did not dent the soul. Our truth was still there, intact, and perhaps we were even more in tune with it.

LIAR, LIAR

As well as being attentive to behavioural patterns of others, revealing hidden truths, we may also be subjected to out-and-out lies spoken aloud. We may have been hurt, burned or left untrusting because someone in our lives has covered up their own story with false statements and inauthentic speech. This is the cause of deep pain.

When you have been lied to it is, of course, very difficult to not take it personally. I have found myself wondering how I've allowed such behaviour into my life. Did I think so badly of myself that I would allow another to lie their way in and out of my story? Probably, otherwise I'm not sure it would have happened. I've been tricked, duped and shat on by people who weren't courageous enough to speak truthfully and, at times, I have felt I may not recover.

Trust often feels like a delicate orb we carry around that, once broken, might never be fixed. When we're lied to, we feel our trust has gone, been smashed to pieces, or taken by another. Yet trust cannot be lost, it's within us always, it just gets covered over by pain and remains dormant until we do the work to repair ourselves from hurt. When we are in touch with our own truth we can then trust again.

At the same time as being angry at myself for trusting those who have lied to me, I'm also weirdly glad of my trusting nature. I'm glad that I've been able to connect with my truth enough to believe in the goodwill of most people. Deep down, I'm wildly optimistic and I want to remain that way – the trade-off is that I may get hurt. Yet I would prefer to be hurt than to be hardened. I would always choose the option that causes pain over closing off my heart altogether.

Those who lie to another's face are suffering. They are papering over wide canyons of their own personal confusion and, usually, guilt. They don't have the tools to work out solutions peacefully or honestly so they create situations that allow them to remain in their seat of power, but it is a fragile kind of power if it is built on lies. If it feels tricky to just sit with the acceptance that someone has lied and caused you pain, I find it helps to remember that the truth will ALWAYS show itself. It cannot be contained forever. It's too powerful and too pure. It will come to light eventually. It could be years after your own pain and suffering have receded but it will surface. Just know that for now.

To be truthful in tricky situations means exposing our vulnerability and many out there are not OK with being vulnerable. They want to feel safe and in power so they lie. If we can break down these situations and see what is really going on we may dig deep enough to find compassion for people who feel they have to lie. I'm not being naive, I know how hard it is to feel kindly towards someone who has lied to you or cheated you. I know the strength it takes to choose compassion over hatred. Again, it's all a choice. We can walk down the road of resentment and blame and weave that into our story for decades – even a lifetime – or we can tiptoe down the road of compassion and the willingness to forgive.

I was discussing this with my lovely mum recently and I asked her how she feels about granting forgiveness. An instant furrowed brow and squint to the eye – 'But what if you just don't feel it?' I know my mum struggles with this one but I still know she is absolutely capable of forgiveness. I still harbour negative feelings towards a handful of people in my life but am willing to walk towards forgiveness. It doesn't feel natural and at times I worry I'll be letting them off the hook if I forgive but, really, I am the only one left suffering if I don't. I'm the one with the tension and upset, not them. So if I forgive them, I free myself.

The first step, I think, is to begin with feeling willing to forgive. Not attempting full-blown acceptance and forgiveness immediately but allowing a gravitational pull towards willingness. If we practise this daily, with repetition, surely it then gets easier to believe and brings us nearer to the real deal?

I also think that we have to forgive ourselves and that is often harder than forgiving anyone else in our lives. We have to forgive ourselves for the mistakes we have made, the truth we've concealed and for allowing in those who have hurt us. I don't think there is a single person who is exempt from needing to learn this one. We all need to forgive ourselves as we have all made mistakes. Forgiveness is the key to letting it all go. The stress, the tension, the physical pain, the worry.

I'm AWFUL at letting go. I'm a control freak in the most

literal sense. I want order and for my stories to make sense so I can then point fingers and feel like I know my place in the world. In those moments of control, I believe I am better than those I am blaming and therefore safe. Nonsense, of course, but we get into habits that make us feel safe. Yet this self-righteousness, while it might feel good for a while, ultimately hinders me from seeing what is real. Letting go of the stories we tell ourselves and our supposed enemies means we have the chance to see the truth clearly.

There are a few people in my life who I find it easy to blame. Obvious metaphorical punch bags that I can pound with anger when I'm feeling irritated. If I take the time to renounce this habitual judgement of mine then I can start to explore what is really going on with me and causing my anger. Sometimes my truth has nothing to do with that person at all. Often, I recognise my anger comes from my own wrongdoings, which I need to work on rather than worrying about what everyone else is up to.

I appreciate there are some people who have lied to us in a way that feels very, very hard to forgive. I KNOW this feeling. In this situation, I can only reach step one: 'the willingness to forgive'. The willingness is there but I'm not completely able to forgive just yet. I'll get there and I'm sure that'll feel pretty amazing when I do but, for now, this is enough. You can't force forgiveness, but you can let it reach you when you are ready.

THE GLITTERING, EFFERVESCENT CIRCUS OF GLAMOUR

There are so many forms of dishonesty in the modern world. In ye olden days, rumours and untruths would have been passed on by word of mouth only, perhaps by letter, but now we can conceal the truth via text, in magazines, email, in the news, emojis and on social media. The opportunities to imbibe and believe lies has multiplied.

The newest place where lies and distortions are spread is of course social media. I'm not about to bash Instagram or Twitter, as the apps themselves are not the problem, it's how we use them. We can create whole fake lives if desired, where we offer snapshots of edited experience to the outside world. We can titivate our lives to look like a glittering, effervescent circus of fun and glamour even when we feel empty inside. We can edit and distil the good bits as if there are no bad bits. We can have multiple forward-slashes in our Instagram bios alerting the world to what a polymath we are even if that's not the reality.

Like most of us, I have believed the myths of social media and have judged myself and compared myself to others. You may know someone who bases their whole social communication with the world on fabrication and inauthenticity. It might wind you up greatly. You might let your eyes roll to the back of your head every time you see one of their highly edited posts. You may feel your truth cannot sit alongside the filtered world of someone who, in real life, you really rather like. I know these are first world problems that we shouldn't lose sleep over but, nevertheless, we are trying to figure out who we are and how truthfully we present ourselves to the world. If those you love, like or simply know are using social media to distract from the truth, can you learn to let it go? Can you look less, judge less and maybe look back to your own truth and ask why you care so much about what someone else is doing? Does it trigger you to feel envious or lacking? Do you worry they might gain outside applause that you feel is unwarranted? For me, it always leads back to comparison. Compare and despair. Even when I know a lot of what I see is fabrication and fantasy, I still use this information to poke and jibe at myself and then sink into self-loathing.

Speaking our truth, and really living it, grants us some healthy detachment from what we see online or on social media. No matter what our eyes rest on we KNOW what we stand for, what our strengths are and what we believe in. We feel no need to compare and no need to sink into self-loathing if we feel we don't match up to high standards.

On good days, I know this to be true. I couldn't care less who has nicer hair, a better job, more popularity, etc. because I'm so deeply rooted to what I know is right for me. My truth tells me to ditch self-punishment and simply view the online fantasy as data that I don't need to act on. On bad days, I'm much more susceptible to the lure of a little self-loathing but writing this book has given me a good chance to look at why. I can see that my habitual behaviour leads me to be very hard on myself, so this is simply another opportunity to do so in moments of weakness. Making better choices for myself allows me to break free from bad habits and ignore the myths of other people's lives. Look online for what makes you glow and feel connected to your own truth. Search for those who inspire and lead the way and hit the like button then.

I've curated a nice world on social media for myself as I follow some cracking people. I've made some amazing friends due to it too. I reunited on Instagram with Annie Price, a documentary maker and campaigner, who I hadn't seen since high school. I didn't know her well at school but remember visiting her house for a play date as a small kid. Since then, we've worked together at my Happy Place Festivals and also on a Sweaty Betty fitness campaign.

Busy Philipps, an amazing actress and online positivity superstar, followed me back on Instagram which led to DM chit-chat and finally meeting up when she landed in London one rainy weekend. She bought me the coolest pair of earrings – little white bunny rabbits perched on hoops – which make me think of LA sunshine every time I wear them.

We connect with, engage with and communicate with authenticity and honesty when we use social media from a place that is true for us. We can all sit and point fingers and also worry about the younger generation in regard to social media but really the responsibility lies with the individual. How do you want to use social media? How does it make you feel? Does it make your truth sing? If not, ditch it. Take back control and be you, and only you, online. And follow those who do the same.

THE TRUTH ALWAYS FLOATS TO THE TOP

When those around us conceal the truth, are too scared to be truthful or out-and-out lie, think back to the moments where you have done the same. Did you lie because you were scared? Did you hide the truth because you weren't at peace with it yourself? Did you choose to not speak up because you were nervous? Did you manipulate a situation because you needed the power? We have all lied or denied our own truth in order to shine, so when those around you are behaving this way, think how best to help them and the situation by remembering what might have helped you in your time of need.

Another thing to bear in mind is that the truth will almost always be revealed, and if you are not being honest you'll have to face the consequences not just of the truth but of lying about it. I know this because, like most explorative and at times rebellious people, I have lied to my mum A LOT. I concealed the truth at the age of twenty-four as I didn't want her knowing I often wandered alone around Camden at 2 a.m. looking for a cab. I hid my truth in my thirties, as at times I was unsure where my career was going myself, so didn't want to worry her with the changes I could feel were going on inside. I have been too scared to tell her things as I haven't wanted to burden her with stress. I only told her about my little cysty friend two weeks after I was diagnosed! Not very on brand with the message of the book!

I once out-and-out lied to my mum when I was getting back with an ex she didn't like. I thought I was running the most covert of missions reigniting the relationship only for her to turn up at my door FOUR HOURS EARLY for a trip to the theatre. She had heard there might be snow on the way so thought she'd better leave 'a little' early to get into town. Cut to the ex-boyfriend hiding in an upstairs bedroom hoping he would find an escape route. Mum instantly smelled a rat. (Why do mums just KNOW when something is up? It's an odd Marvel superhero skill they all have.) I kept adamantly stating nothing was up until she decided she didn't want to just sit and chat and instead would go and clean my bathroom, UPSTAIRS! At the time, I was in my late twenties and had moved out a decade ago – why on earth did she want to clean my bathroom? SHE KNEW! You can guess the end of the story. Cross mum, embarrassed ex-boyfriend, pissed-off me. The lesson learned here is that the truth always floats to the top. ESPECIALLY with mums! They seem to have a supersonic power of extracting the truth from us which makes it even dicier to try to withhold it.

When those around us are not speaking their truth, we have choices. We can choose to act as a positive catalyst to help them reveal their truth – by listening, by offering a safe space, by letting them know we are there for them. Or we can simply feel safe remembering that, if we are being lied to, the truth will show itself at some point. Knowing the truth will emerge might just give us the strength to get through tough times where we feel we have been duped. The truth always floats to the top!

Think of five lies you tell yourself, and one lie you have told others.

_____

_____

_____

_____

_____

_____

_____

_____

Have you been found out? Was the lie worse than the truth you were hiding?

_____

_____

_____

_____

_____

_____

_____

_____

8

HOW DO WE STAY TRUTHFUL IN A WORLD THAT OFTEN LIES?

Weeding out the truth from the lies is tough. The world today is more densely populated and runs at a faster speed than ever before and can feel very noisy. To stay focused on our truth may feel hard; we are like little satellite dishes transmitting and receiving information all day long. Some of this information we need, some we don't, some we really shouldn't engage with. We have our phones, newspapers, TV adverts, sidebar adverts, books, magazines, YouTube, search engines, WhatsApp groups. The noise is inescapable and frequently overwhelming. We believe so much without question and form fixed opinions on society, culture, our friends, leaders, communities and ourselves on the basis of conflated information and scraps of the truth.

The catalyst for writing this book was of course finding out about Mr Cyst rock climbing up the face of my vocal cords. He is possibly there because I don't speak my truth often enough. I find it hard. We all find it hard. Not because we are weak or incapable but because the modern world makes it hard.

The world is often presented to us as a scary place full of danger and threat. Transgression, segregation and lies ubiquitous. We are taught to be scared and to stay in line. The TV says so, our phones say so, the papers say so. We often fall in line, do what is expected of us and keep quiet as we fear judgement or being alone in opinion and voice. I've sucked on throat sweets, coated my vocal cords with overpriced manuka honey and rested my voice during the day when I'm writing, yet I know deep down that this little throat critter will not leave me until I really get to the root of the problem. No one is going to help me on this one. I'm going to have to make better choices when it comes to what I digest, who I listen to and who I go to for inspiration. It might not feel like we have much choice but there are ways for us to distil and edit how much fear we take on and which sources of information feel right for us.

THE TRUTH AND NOTHING BUT THE TRUTH

How do we decipher how much of what we digest is really the truth? If I think about this one too much I start to feel very anxious and tense. I'm not going to go off on a political rampage as that is not why you have picked up this book (head to the 'M' section of your local bookshop and look for

Andrew Marr for that), but we all know how little of the truth we are often fed even by the people running whole countries. We are thrown small morsels of information that could sway us to vote in a particular way but rarely feel fully informed. I think that's why so many countries have problems with voter apathy. It's not because people feel like they can't be bothered to vote, it's because they don't feel they know enough because they haven't been properly informed.

I've heard numerous conspiracy theories in the last few weeks about the Covid-19 pandemic. The rumour mills are working overtime and the most far-out theories are being discussed because we don't always trust what we are being fed from the top. Anxiety is high because we don't feel safe, and not feeling safe is usually due to not knowing enough. A lack of information or a distrust in leaders is leaving us feeling vulnerable and unsure. The word 'uncertainty' has been used more times this year than in the history of modern language because many don't trust what we are being told. OK, that's enough on politics, we don't want Andrew getting scared.

Whether we're politically engaged or not, the onslaught of negative news means we often see the world through very pessimistic eyes. Newspapers know that fear sells and we become used to hearing the most horrific stories every day. We find ourselves reading fearmongering articles, looking at terrifying pictures and using these to make decisions about our own lives. My mother often hands me dog-eared scraps she has carefully extracted from newspapers offering up advice on how to avoid the latest wave of local crime, or which foods I should definitely now steer clear of. Lin Cotton is a natural worrier, so these sorts of page-fillers leap out at her and give fuel to her underlying concern about the world around her. As any dutiful mother might, she feels the urgent need to pass them all on to me. And who can blame dear Mamma Cotton? Daily, we are being told to be scared, yet we forget that a lot of what we hear might not be true.

Of course, we cannot lead ignorant lives and pretend we all live in fairyland where only good stuff happens, but the balance is definitely off. It has been interesting that, as countries around the world go into lockdown, we are seeing a surge in positive stories as we all seek reassurance – whether that's Italians singing from their balconies, whole streets out clapping at sunset for the brave NHS and care workers or people on social media genuinely finding fun in the ordinary and basic. Because the news has been so harrowing of late and so scary at times, the good news has upped its game too. I so hope the positive stories are still making the headlines once the pandemic is over.

I acknowledge that it is important we know that others are suffering and where there is injustice afoot so we can have empathy and perhaps even try to help but we need to see the good stuff too. Otherwise we are being sold a constant daily lie that only bad stuff is happening out there. Hands up who was also born in the 1980s (or before)? As well as Hypercolor T-shirts and jelly shoes you may also remember being allowed to cycle to your local park on your own. I was allowed so much freedom, like many kids were before the internet was born. The newspapers still churned out some pretty negative and fearmongering stories but there was less of it. More of a chance to avoid it if you chose to. There were no phone alerts from news websites prompting you to take an instant look at the latest terrifying events on planet earth. I regularly jumped on my pink Candy bike and went down to the local park with my mate Becky Currie – and note, this without the supposed safety net of a mobile phone. I would just go off and have some wild park-life fun and then come home roughly when I told Mum I would be back for my tea (Alphabites and beans, obvs). That was normal then and I don't think it is now.

My son is seven, exactly the age where I was allowed to cycle up and down my suburban street alone and I would no way let Rex out the front door to go explore solo. I actually find myself getting anxious when out and about with Rex and Honey as I feel I can't take my eyes off either of them. For many parents, this panicky attentiveness has become the new normal and so much of it is down to how we ingest news. We've heard so many horrific stories and the fear has been ramped up.

I don't think there are any more humans capable of terrible things today than there have been throughout history, but we certainly hear of it a lot more. We believe that the world is a scarier place and that we have to be vigilant in case someone hacks our laptops, steals our chained-up bike, scams us when booking a holiday, rifles through our backpack when we're not looking, as if there is more crime and more worry than ever before. But is that the truth?

My belief is that there is a balance throughout the world, and perhaps throughout history, between the good and the bad. Maybe the balance isn't exactly 50/50, but there's a rough balance of good stuff and bad and that usually spills into our own lives too. For every story of a life lost, we have a story of a courageous doctor or nurse. For every bullied teen, we have a heartwarming story of connection. For every selfish, criminal act we read about, we have a tale of inspiring altruism. We get a bit of both. Yet if we only hear of the bad we start to think we live in a scary world and that means we think fear is the appropriate response to the world around us.

I find this one so difficult to live with since I became a parent. I'm not saying that those without kids won't feel the pressure of our supposedly scary world but, for me, having kids has made me much more susceptible to the fearmongering present in our daily culture. It puts me on high alert and often robs me of being in the moment. I'm constantly trying to plan ahead to ward off danger. I use my mapped-out iCal as a shield from any unknown scary shit on the horizon, each day marked with events to trick myself into thinking I know what is around the corner. I find myself believing the lie shown to me every day that the world is scary, yet I know deep down that my own truth is a trusting one. I battle against the headlines and round-robin emails from friends warning me of the latest scam and try to remember that I am a trusting person. Not a foolish one – a practical and trusting one. I so often forget this about myself and get carried away by a white-water current of fear. I catastrophise and find ways to validate my fear. I actually go and seek it out as that usually feels easier than trying to combat my panic with grounded trust.

Most of us have had to take a good look at trust and hope this year. The world-stopping pandemic that is speedily coursing over the planet is uncharted territory for us. Before this happened, we may have felt that we were prepared for the unexpected. After all, we buy insurance for trips abroad to cover any eventualities. We pay out big sums to insurance companies just in case we were one day to be burgled or have our house subside due to moist British earth. Yet nothing could have prepared us for this. None of us saw a global pandemic being a reality. It's a movie script too far out to be believed. It is the unthinkable and certainly something not to be entertained as reality. So now we are IN IT how do we have hope? Our worst nightmares have come true and we have to keep on digging around, searching for our hope among the piled-up laundry and yet-to-be-filled-in home-schooling worksheets.

I think most of us have not been able to truly think about hope during this time but instead have surrendered to living in the moment. It's as if we've realised the best way not to succumb to fear is to take this experience minute by minute. We don't know when it will all end, we don't know when lockdown will be lifted, we don't know when schools will reopen (please soon! I'm a useless teacher!), we don't know when the economy will pick itself back up, we don't know if we will ever be or feel the same again. Hope seems at times unattainable because our lives look so different to usual, so instead we resist full-on fear by being in the NOW. Get up, drink coffee, try to think of something fun to do at home with the kids, cook food with leftovers, smile at neighbours, cook more food, watch TV, read books, bed. The days are split into manageable portions that allow us to feel we have some control over this chaos. I truly believe that this moment-by-moment living is an act of hope in itself, even if many of us don't feel we can grab full-throttle hope at this point.

We can stop reading the papers and stop listening to the news and actively seek out stories that feel more nourishing, but some would argue that is blinkered and selfish, and right now it is hard to avoid the news altogether. Or we can give ourselves rules about how much we can digest and how much we will choose to believe. I'm trying to listen to my own barometer of what I can handle each day. Some days I feel more hopeful, so watching the news or reading online articles is manageable. On other days I need all the funny memes I can find. I need good, gentle novels at night and a heavy dose of TikTok videos from my mate Clare. I gauge it on the day and try not to beat myself up for not being able to handle watching the news every night.

We will all have a different outlook on this one as we all have varying personal limits. Some of us will be experiencing high levels of stress in our everyday lives due to our personal circumstances and perhaps will therefore need a total detoxification of all extraneous negativity. Some of us may be living a more peaceful life and feel we can cope with taking it on and perhaps even acting on it, by volunteering or fundraising or simply raising awareness. My brilliant mate Suzie has been volunteering in a London hospital throughout the pandemic. Go Suzie! Remembering we have a choice about what we absorb from the media is imperative. There is no right or wrong, but there is a truth that will be right for you.

DON'T LET YOUR OPTIMISM DWINDLE

I think that culturally we have become more pessimistic due to the way we download so much information from the outside world. We can come to see optimism as foolish or whimsical, or even blinkered from reality. I was chatting to a nature expert recently who said he was wildly optimistic about our planet. He had great hope we would, as a human race, be able to turn around the terrible situation we've gotten ourselves into environmentally. He had confidence that we can change the ways in which we have robbed our planet of its resources. It struck me that he is the first person I have heard say this. We only hear about how badly everything is going. Of course, we need this awareness of the bad news so the likes of the indomitable Greta Thunberg can lead great revolution, but is it wrong to allow a little hope in too? Surely with a little optimism we have more of an impetus to make change, as hope allows us to fundamentally believe it is possible?

Feeling that optimism is frivolous in the face of bad news is an example of how we allow today's culture to warp our truth. If you know you are optimistic by nature (and I think most of us are, as that's how we start off as children) then how much do you allow the outside world to meddle with that? I do quite frequently. I heard someone recently say that they had heard that our recycling doesn't even get recycled. WHAT?! New panic alert! I usually carefully arrange my waste in colour-coded boxes, optimistically waving it off to be recycled. Now I have to worry that it isn't being recycled at all? Clearly I've never chased the recycling truck down the road to the recycling plant and then followed that waste to the mythical recycling factory where new products are made. I have to have hope that they are but now I also feel worried about every bit of plastic I buy. My naturally trusting ways have been floored by a conspiracy theory floating around.

It's hard to live authentically and truthfully today as we aren't helped very much by those in positions to make great change. How many petitions have we seen signed and sent to supermarkets begging them to sell all their fruit and veg loose instead of in plastic? How many of the supermarkets have followed up on it? Not many. We can each do our bit and make good choices we know feel right to us but we are not always supported from the top. I'm sure no one would argue if the government put a ban on the creation of any un-recyclable plastic (i.e. salad bags, tear-off seals on fruit punnets etc.), but they haven't, so instead we often feel we have little choice but to buy our products in the packaging provided. When that makes us feel powerless to make change, it is harder to be optimistic, but maybe we are still allowed a little hope for future change. Even collective hope that could lead to more action?

These are all thoughts I ponder daily. It's a shame so many of us think, 'What's the point of living my truth if it is seemingly so bloody hard?' Yet I totally understand why. It isn't realistic in the modern world for us all to grow our own fruit and veg and to never buy anything new ever again. The world, and how it works, has changed so much. We are all simply scrambling around trying to keep up with it.

LEARNING FROM NATURE

In modern life, we often feel disconnected from nature, which is a huge problem for all of us. Work, school and other commitments mean there are fewer opportunities to be in nature, especially if you live in a city, as time whizzes by in a flurry of unanswered emails and phone pings. We feel we haven't got the time or space to get out into the natural world and then a life disconnected from nature becomes our new normal.

The modern world often tells us we don't need nature. Instead of sitting under a tree, perhaps we need that new hairdryer that looks like a small tennis racket and dries your hair in 3.5 seconds? We don't need the elements but might be tempted by the comfort of a ready meal that takes four minutes to cook and tastes like salt that'll leave you wanting more. We lose our sense of ourselves as part of nature and we lose nature from our daily lives.

I battle with this one constantly. I know my truth aligns with nature, I know I can learn so much from it, but I get distracted by other demands on my time. This morning I went for a run and it was tough; tough but essential. Usually the tough things are. I had anger in me (I know! Again!) and it felt like it needed to escape my crooked shoulders and tense jaw. I ran against the wind with Royal Blood playing loudly in my headphones. The adrenalin kicked in and pulsed through my muscles, allowing them to push against the wind's mighty strength. Rage fired up my chest and fast-beating heart, giving me the freedom to move my limbs and exorcise the anger. The dominant easterly wind allowed me to work through something and use my body to physically move on from a tricky emotion.

This experience reminded me that we should feel the elements often. We should allow our bodies to feel cold, hot, pushed about by gales, rained on, tingled by ice. We need to feel it all and allow our bodies to strengthen due to discomfort. The modern world tells us to avoid the elements and keep warm, dry, cool and unbothered with the latest clothing, hot water bottle, umbrella, heated car, etc.

This morning's run wasn't comfortable by any means. I would much rather have been in a warm bath reading a book but the discomfort and full-bodied experience of running with the wind was what my truth needed. I needed the anger to move on to allow my inner calm to flourish for the rest of the day. I'm not always this virtuous and of course I sometimes pick a warm bath and a face pack over nature and that's fine too. This morning, though, I needed howling winds and muscle burn to get back to my truth.

We can learn so much from observing nature but instead we type into search engines for answers. We worry about why we feel so awful but forget to look at the seasons to be reminded that, like the seasons, we are always changing and adjusting and adapting. We panic that our kids are too shouty, angry, moany, disobedient without looking to growth in nature to remind us that becoming mature is a process that requires patience. We think the modern world has all of the answers but in fact it is taking us away from what we intuitively know and what nature can teach us.

Is there any part of your life where you feel ill at ease? Where you have lost the ability to root back to your truth and work through stuff? Can you look at nature to see if it can offer up any thoughts or solutions? Let me elaborate. I have had relationships over the years that felt very unbalanced. I have struggled immensely with a certain dynamic and wondered why I'm putting in 100 per cent yet the other is giving very little at all. I'm a 100 per cent person and always have been. I cannot give 70 per cent effort with anything. This can be brilliant but also massively to my detriment. 100 per cent isn't always the best. Sometimes 60 per cent is so much better – more relaxed, less desperate, and leaves something for you at the end. I know this; nevertheless, I'm 100 per cent nearly 100 per cent of the time. Exhausting. In these moments of imbalance, I have allowed anger to reign and have climbed atop a sturdy horse to remain in a lofty position of righteousness. If in those moments I could look to nature I might find some solace or even a solution.

Nature IS balance. There has to be balance for anything to grow. The correct ratio of shade to sunlight. The right pH balance in the earth itself. The right balance of water to enable growth. If I am overwatering a situation, oversaturating a person with my own sunlight, I have already shaken the balance of the pH in the soil. If I want balance, I can see from nature that I have to pull back a little. I have to give less so the other can give more. I have to allow the other person involved the opportunity to put some work in. If I am doing it all they cannot. This is a lesson I have to learn again and again as I'm a people-pleasing, overachieving, Virgo control freak. I have to pull back that watering can and wait for the rain. The modern world could perhaps offer me up therapists or online articles on relationship dynamics but the truth also lies in nature.

CHANGES AND LIBERATION

There was a time not long ago when most of the world did not believe love was for everyone. Laws existed (and unfortunately still do in some countries) forbidding same-sex love from being legally recognised. It was only in the last century that male homosexuality was decriminalised throughout England and Wales, with Scotland and Northern Ireland following suit later on. The same-sex marriage act was only passed in 2013 with the first couple legally marrying in 2014. That was basically yesterday! Years of suppression for so many because the world did not recognise their truth. The people in power made love OK for some but not others.

In any situation where suppression is forced and truth is limited en masse, the struggle and pain feel insurmountable but perhaps a little faith can be gained from knowing that these beliefs change. It is reassuring to remember this, when the lies we are presented with in the modern world might seem fixed, indestructible and downright depressing. Take hope from seeing lies that have been busted and exposed and overcome.

There have been times throughout history when, for reasons of skin colour, religion, sexuality or gender, whole communities have been suppressed. The prejudiced beliefs of those in power, whether political, religious or cultural, have seeped through to indoctrinate the masses and in turn made many lose sight of their own individual truth. Historically, many have been swayed by popular opinion and peer pressure to align with the status quo even when at odds with their personal truth. We either didn't speak up against suppression or chose to look the other way. We are obviously and painfully still working through this problem, seen at the time of writing with the horrific murder of George Floyd in Minneapolis.

This event provided a stark reminder that huge, essential change is still needed, and for that to happen we need to take action. When the news broke and our screens were flooded with horrific images of injustice I felt terribly sad and confused. My blind spots appeared with more clarity than ever before. Without noise, action and continued conversation this will continue happening globally every day. I had previously thought my not being racist was enough. That believing in equality for all was enough. I now understand that it wasn't, and isn't. Active anti-racism is the only way forward to create proper long-lasting change.

Speaking up and demanding change is the only way that we can challenge racism and stand in the way of systemic racism. I've been walking around knowing I am not racist but I have not taken enough action. I have always tried to give space to a diverse group of interesting people on the Happy Place podcast and at the Happy Place Festival but I recognise that I need to do more. I have more work to do and I have more listening and learning ahead of me.

For systemic racism to end we all need to shout loudly and use the influence we have in the areas where we can make change. We can speak to our children's head teachers and ask them to include black history in the curriculum. We can teach our children at home about important figures in black history, music, art, film and philanthropy. We can read books and discuss what we've learned. We can use social media to spread awareness of inspirational black people who are making great change. We can look to work with and employ a diverse group of individuals. Look at your life and think about where you can make your own changes.

This year has been challenging for so many reasons and many of us are waking up to truths in double-quick time because they're coming at us thick and fast. Death, loss, injustice, sickness, lockdown, job loss, furlough, collapsing businesses, isolation, fear: we've had a lot to digest in a short time but it's peeling our eyes open to our truth and also to a global truth. We can dare to hope for great, positive change in our lives, and the lives of others, as a result of the pandemic and the discussion around racial equality, yet that does not mean that getting to this point has been comfortable. As I've discussed previously, discovering the truth and then making moves for change can feel far from comfortable. We have to go through great internal inventory to excavate all of our worries, fears, shame and hurt and then create new methods and neural pathways to carry us down the bumpy road of newness. During the Black Lives Matter movement of 2020 I felt uncomfortable and anxious, yet desperate to help with change. Recently I was messaging Jay Shetty, the renowned speaker and writer, about discomfort and he imparted a brilliant piece of advice that I've been focusing on ever since. He told me that to run from discomfort to comfort is what actually makes us unhappy. As counterintuitive as it may seem, sitting in discomfort is always the best way to contentment. How many times have you run from discomfort straight to the cake tin? I've done this so many times. I've itched with discomfort and wanted to crawl out of my skin, so instead of sitting with it I have binge-watched bad TV, or spent mind-numbing hours on Pinterest. Yet to SIT in that discomfort, to make friends with it and genuinely learn from the experience, is probably the best way to feel truly alive.

There is so much we can do in order to speak our truth very loudly on this matter. As I write this book we are deep in a truly global conversation about race. Every radio show is discussing it and presenting new thoughts on how we can move forward. Social media is leading us to interesting people who can educate us further. Marches are stomping across our cities with fists pumping the air, charging each molecule with the energy of change. Thousands of voices chant the truth through the summer air, demanding to be heard. Not only do we have to speak our truth but we really, really have to listen to it as well.

Another societal challenge has been to open our eyes and look at gender. Historically in the western world only two genders were recognised, male and female, and each had clearly defined roles imposed on them. Of course, there are records of trans people throughout history the world over, yet commonly the more restrictive, traditional roles of gender have perhaps been understood and accepted more readily. Women had roles as wives and mothers, suitable hobbies, appropriate passions, a manner that was deemed feminine, etc. The same went for men. A list was drawn up over the years of what men should do, wear, say and how they should demonstrate their emotions. But in recent times, not only have we understood how damaging this rigid sense of gender roles is for individuals but we've also been liberated by losing the boundaries and acknowledging a whole never-ending rainbow of bespoke definitions of gender and sexuality. It seems this is the natural cycle of how we try to unpick the structures we are taught. We unlearn them.

At the turn of the twentieth century, the structure under question was the suppression of women and the lie that females weren't worthy of voting. The suffragettes tore apart this theory and fought for change. Their truth and deep knowing, against the laws of the time, gave them courage to stand up and speak up to challenge the lies that oppressed them. In the 1950s and 60s, the brutal segregation of race in the United States was challenged by trailblazers like Martin Luther King and other civil rights activists. Martin Luther King's life truth was captured and immortalised in the form of his beautiful, poetic and powerful 'I Have a Dream' speech, which led to societal change. More recently here in the UK and Ireland, author and speaker Reni Eddo-Lodge, writer and musician Akala, academic and author Emma Dabiri and many others make it their mission to keep change moving in the right direction. In the last half of the twentieth century, sexual orientation was challenged with many publicly opening up about their truth. Many made a stand and exposed themselves to judgement from the ignorant and fearful because the truth was far too powerful to stay quiet.

It makes us feel hopeful to see these positive changes from history, but there is still a long way to go for many people who feel marginalised and who are told by sections of society that they don't belong. I like to think that the seminal moments like the civil rights movement, #BlackLivesMatter and the George Floyd protests can be considered as a kind of cultural 'Big Bang' – an explosion that is necessary for everyone to stop and look and take note of the injustice that is present. Then the hard work really begins and, in most cases, must be continued by each generation.

In these moments of global struggle, communities form naturally in adversity. Speaking the truth is hard but many people speaking as one makes it harder to ignore what's being said. The need to speak up can seem contagious, but that doesn't make it any less hard for those brave enough to do it. The confidence to speak up is passed on from individual to individual and then groups are formed who have a louder voice in numbers. As we all know from personal experience, speaking one's truth is hard work and putting wheels in motion often even harder, but in numbers great things can be achieved.

Look at Greta Thunberg, once a lone student sat outside the Swedish parliament to protest climate change, but now bringing together millions of kids to join hands and hearts in the name of saving the planet. One person has created a global movement of positive thinking and hope.

Of course, unfair bias, prejudice and bigotry still exist in the world, and they likely always will. But the truth tellers will also exist, speaking out against lies and taking action to challenge them. The work is never-ending but each time we witness brave souls standing up to have their say, we can join forces with them or, at the very least, feel inspired enough to speak our own truth too.

CHALLENGING THE LAW AND ERIC'S SMILE

One of our relatives was recently forced to challenge a law he felt was unjust and unfair when faced with a matter of life or death.

My husband Jesse has a bevy of the most wonderful cousins, the Findlays. Standing in a room with all of them, there is a cacophony of laughter and non-stop chat and there's a similarity in their faces that you can't ignore. They welcomed me with open arms from the minute I met them at Jesse's great-nanna Patricia's birthday lunch. One particular smiley, heart-shaped face belonged to Eric Findlay. The same age as me with two beautiful children and an incredible wife, Mo. I'm not sure I've met a more happy-go-lucky character. Eric had a beautiful, understated confidence that allowed his eccentricity to shine through.

In 2019, we received a phone call from Jesse's uncle Eric telling us that Eric junior was sick and it wasn't looking good. It's the sort of out-of-the-blue news that shocks you to the core. Your body feels weightless and unanchored and words don't make sense. It hit everybody hard. The whole family was suddenly looking at a very different future and this of course hit Ben, Eric's closest brother and business partner. They had grown up thick as thieves and remained the closest friends as well as siblings. They were the perfect balance in family life and business, knowing exactly who had what skill and how to use it. As soon as he heard the news, Ben got to work thinking of solutions and ways to help his brother and young family.

He started to research CBD oil and the benefits of taking micro-doses of the oil containing the illegal substance THC. Cannabis oil is now widely sold and you can find it in drop form, in face creams and even biscuits, but these products are legal because the THC has been extracted. THC is the bit that is more commonly associated with smoking and getting high. The more Ben looked into the benefits of THC for Eric's illness, the more convinced he became of its benefits. He read so many stories of people managing their pain with THC and even healing from life-threatening illness. His truth said, 'GO FOR IT'; the law said 'NO'.

Ben set about illegally sourcing cannabis plants that contained THC so he could set up his own lab at home to make an oil that could help with Eric's diagnosis and pain. He risked getting caught and prosecuted but that threat felt insignificant when he thought of helping his brother. The last few weeks of Eric's life were enhanced greatly due to Ben's home-brewed oil which offered him a little comfort and pain relief.

Eric peacefully passed away in May 2019. His smile and sense of adventure will never be forgotten and Ben continues to drive to change laws as a tribute. In his brother's memory, he wants to do some good and help give people in a similar situation another option. He recently appeared on the BBC talking about his choices, again putting himself at risk, but often in life-changing situations like this, the truth cannot be restrained. Ben's truth is now to talk and to help others in a similar situation and that is a very powerful thing.

MAKE IT YOUR NEW NORMAL

When the world seems to be against us we have two options. To retreat and suppress our truth or to stand up and speak. Standing up and speaking out is not the easy choice. I may not have faced life or death decisions, but I have made great changes to my own life and stood up to people who have told me I'm worthless. I haven't always made this point face-to-face in the moment, but I feel that so much of the work I do today is my way of showing those who have bullied and humiliated me that I have a voice and I'm not afraid to use it. For every time I've been told I am bad, shit, annoying (they're never particularly creative disses), I have stood up and shouted a little louder. I've been even more honest in telling the world who I am and even more confident in doing what I believe is right. It took me years to understand that I didn't just have to take it, that I could push against what I was told by the small group of outsiders who felt the need to discuss me in a negative way. These days I have a comprehensive understanding of what a waste of time it is to do otherwise.

I can only offer up small examples from my own life but there are of course so many people out there who put their safety on the line, stand up in the face of adversity or continue to dedicate their lives to their truth. Seek them out, read positive stories about people doing good things. Digest more powerful storytelling rather than mindless gossip. Feel fired up by those who stand confidently with their truth rather than lacking as a result of comparing yourself to your peers. These are all mantras I have to remind myself of constantly.

I know that digesting positive, empowering stories about other people's truths will serve me so much better than downing endless supplies of gossip and fear. I have to make it my new normal.

MY FAVOURITE TRUTH TELLERS

Here are eight truth tellers who I look up to for inspiration and empowerment when the world seems like a hard place.

★ **Eckhart Tolle.** Whenever the world gets too noisy and confusing for me I have to have grounded, simple wisdom so Eckhart is my man. His calm, thoughtful, yet assured tone always makes me feel less panicked and a lot more connected to the truth.

★ **Erling Kagge** is an amazing explorer and writer who I have befriended in recent years. His books bring me headspace and a connection to what is real.

★ **My brother Jamie.** He is my very own London Eckhart who I can actually call up for advice. He never reacts without thought or judges. He is the coolest, calmest person you'll ever meet and always offers up a snippet of considered advice that allows me to make better decisions.

★ **Judith Heumann.** Judith is an American disability rights activist who has been a driving force behind the human rights legislation and policies including and benefitting the disability community. I discovered her through the exceptional documentary *Crip Camp* and am greatly inspired by her and how she has spoken out.

★ **Holly Tucker** is the most sensational force of nature and has inspired me in my business life for some time. She is a working mum who has built an entrepreneurial career from the ground up so I always go to her for advice on what move to make next. She is experienced and loves to help people and will always tell the truth.

★ **Oprah.** An obvious one but she will always inspire me. She has created a life and powerful career out of truth-telling. She was one of the first TV hosts to be brutally honest about her own story and then use it to forge connection with people from all walks of life. I will love her forever.

★ **Elizabeth Gilbert.** Her writing has guided me personally and also pushed me to be more honest in how I write. I have loved every word she has put to paper and will continue being inspired by her for life. As her life story unfolds, she tells it how it is.

★ **My parents.** They constantly inspire me to dig deeper, get even more honest and dance to my own beat. Whether they encourage me or challenge me I will always come to the same conclusion – that aiming to be 100 per cent me is the right option.

Who are your inspirations?

_____

_____

_____

_____

_____

_____

_____

_____

_____

_____

_____

_____

_____

_____

_____

_____

_____

_____

_____

_____

9

WHAT IF MY TRUTH CHANGES?

Ah, now I've been slightly putting off writing this chapter, as I think I'm in the middle of great personal change now. Change, to a control freak like me, is a rainstorm to a fresh blow-dry. I feel the ground shifting beneath my feet when change is on the cards as I know I can't rely on my many lists, phone notes and tidy office to keep me feeling safe. I have to let go and tentatively step into the unknown.

My truth has shifted greatly in many ways in the last five years. A lot of these changes have expanded my way of thinking and brought new, exciting people into my life, yet other bits have felt tricky and uncertain. For so long, my truth was to follow the dream of being a TV personality. To chase the big jobs with big audiences and shouty, headline-grabbing press surrounding them. That equalled success to me. I defined myself as a TV and radio presenter, both because it made me feel like I was headed somewhere and because it was easy for others to understand. I was in a clearly drawn box that I liked, and that others celebrated, because apparently that's what happens when you're on TV.

Here's the tricky bit: over the last few years I have slowly been less drawn to the jobs I had become known for. I started feeling more and more physically uncomfortable with the roles I was taking on and started to question if I was right for them at all. The more uncomfortable I felt, the less I got asked to do them. As I sit here today, I haven't been asked to host a TV show in over a year. I've been taken off (OK, sacked) from so many TV jobs over the last five years that I've lost count.

I'm finding this hard to type as we are so conditioned to only tell others about how great we are and how loved we are to ensure more of the same, but hey, that's not the truth and we are ONLY speaking the truth here. If you judge me, or others judge me because I'm revealing my fallibility then so be it.

During this transition and the slow uncovering of my own truth, I felt at first very dented by the lack of TV work. I felt unloved and started to wonder what was wrong with me. Why were all of my peers getting jobs left, right and centre but not me? Was I faulty? Annoying? Dressing incorrectly? Asking the wrong questions? Or maybe, just maybe, this is a new path for me. My truth is exposing what I really enjoy and making space for more of it.

At the time of writing my podcast has had 33 million downloads, we are working up new Happy Place Festival ideas, running Happy Place charity initiatives and engaging with people who are equally as excited about it as we are, yet many people don't know what I do anymore. How do you describe me? As a TV presenter who doesn't do TV? Radio host who does bits and bobs? Writer? Yes, that's a bit of it. I don't really fit into a neat box anymore.

Occasionally, I get caught in a hangover of what I used to deem my truth. I used to believe that TV equalled success. Being seen was what made people connect with me. Now, thanks to really working with my truth and wanting to dive fully into the world of mental health, wellbeing and deep conversation, I have to let a lot of old ideals go. Last week I was told that a TV show I had presented would be coming back – without me. My instant reaction was a feeling of not quite being good enough but then a thought came . . . maybe this is a chance for even more of my truth to be revealed. Maybe this is a chance to be at home with my kids even more but also a chance to explore new ways to bring Happy Place to life. Maybe my truth just won't have it any other way?

The same day that I was dumped off the TV show, I went to a yoga class. My husband demanded I go and get some clarity, because he knows yoga gives me headspace and helps me gain perspective. He put the kids to bed as I scurried up the road in the rain to the yoga studio. The brilliant teacher Tim started the class by speaking about how we need to trust the person that we know we are, not the person we believe we should be. OH WOW! BANG! BONG! Resonating central! I grabbed hold of that notion and yoga'd the hell out of it for the next hour.

When your truth changes, you have to let go of old ideas about yourself and stop worrying what everyone else will think about your decisions. Some might not see what I do as being as successful as the achievements of my TV presenter peers. They might think it less exciting but it matters not. I have to rid myself of old tags and definitions and go with what feels right. Even more change is on the horizon, I can feel it. I just need to sit back and let go!

THE CHAMELEON YEARS

If I look back over my twenties, I can see how often it felt like my truth changed and how I outwardly showed the world I was moving with it. My hair colour changed every few months to cover my insecurity. Thick, smudged black eyeliner covered the fear of being me. Although I believe my inner truth (and yours) is something deep and unchanging, the way I live it and express it has changed and developed over time, and is still doing so today. When I look back at my life, my ideas about who I was are radically different to what they are today, which can be surprising to look back on.

Like most, there was a period where I was full of lust and fantasy and truly believed another person was capable of completing me. I thought a boy could perhaps unlock my hidden beauty and self-worth and had no clue it was already there within me. This sort of dynamic made me feel I had to be whatever the male needed. Fun? Sure, I can do fun! I hate parties but I can dance on the table and stay up way later than I want to. Quiet and compliant? Absolutely, I can do that! I can quell my need to talk through any silence and act like the dainty, feminine fairy you need me to be. Supportive? Oh, now I'm an expert at this one! I can put my every feeling and worry aside to make sure you feel OK at all times. I can put up with your lack of attention and communication rather than rocking the boat by expressing any needs of my own.

At the time, I didn't see how I could just be me, speak my truth and keep hold of a boyfriend. Maybe I wouldn't have kept hold of any of the ones I was dating but I'm not sure that would have been such a bad thing.

Now I'm older, I still seek that sense of love and want to bring out the best in myself but the shape of that truth looks different. These days, I prize honest communication, boundary setting and understanding. It is about being 100 per cent me without any reduction, morphing or change. I only reached this much-needed epiphany because it got so bloody boring doing it the other way. It got so tiresome to keep changing my favourite band due to the guy I was dating. It got SO boring watching the films they wanted to watch and talking about things that only interested them. I was so scared to have an opinion or speak my truth in case it was 'wrong'.

Accessing my truth meant changing these ideas about myself and developing a deeper understanding of my own self-worth. It also meant a lot of regret that I had let so many walk over me previously. When we change, we often look back at our questionable actions from the past and wonder, 'Why?' I believe these moments of often painful transition through change are the times in which we learn the most. We learn about our own strength, emotional intelligence and resilience.

UNBREAKABLE LOVE

We all wish that love was permanent and unbreakable. We place all our hope, effort and future in the hands of love and hope for the best. Our truth tells us that we should throw everything into the relationship and tell the world about it too, yet our feelings can change, though that doesn't feel possible in the throes of new love. We wholeheartedly believe love is endless, enduring, unbreakable, shatterproof. This love feels like our truth. And I believe it is our truth, for a bit, but then it changes.

Before I met my husband, I was engaged to someone else. Another Jesse – I know, what are the fucking chances! A wedding venue was booked. A family ring perched on my wedding finger ready for a life of harmony. Both of us (and I'll be careful how I tell this story because I can only speak for myself, not for him) thought this was it. Our truth was togetherness and matrimony. Then our truth changed. On an April afternoon when unspoken frustrations were fired off in angry tones, things shifted for good. A day later, our truth was something completely new and different: separation, cancellation of a wedding venue, the returning of a grandmother's ring.

After this kind of life-changing event the future can look empty and pretty scary. For a while, I felt as if I were free-falling but I was able to sense my truth when I spent time with the people who loved me. A holiday with my close friend Laura was enough to help me back on my feet. She was the person who could bring out my best bits and make me feel alive, and it was good to be reminded I didn't need a partner for that. There is no animosity between me and the other Jesse today and I'm very happy that he is married with a little girl and is living his brilliant truth.

THE PAIN OF CHANGE AND NEW NORMALS

Relationship breakdowns are hard to navigate and we often feel we have lost all sense of self in these moments. Our personality and purpose seem so woven around the other person in the relationship – then the 'our' becomes 'my' and the 'us' becomes 'me'. When it's over, we have to work out new ways to get back to our truth on our own.

How easily you get back on your feet will depend on how much you relied on the other. Maybe there will even be liberation in that rediscovery of your own independent self. Perhaps you'll feel free to make choices and more relaxed knowing you have room to explore parts of life you had parked previously.

Our expression of our truth changes shape over time and with that can come loss. I think, from experience, we need to remember that loss is usually temporary. We may call off a wedding, split up from a partner, end a marriage, leave a job, end a friendship, move location and all seems lost but ultimately we still have our hearts, our love and our knowledge. They are ours for the keeping – they are our truth. We still have our lungs to breathe in adventure and newness. We still have the unknown in front of us to explore. Change is painful; we all know that and yet change very rarely lasts for long. New rhythms set in and what was once different and unknown starts to feel, well . . . quite normal.

Our truth changing shape means those around us might need to change too. Remember leaving home? Maybe you haven't yet, so this is to come. But it's a big, life-defining moment for all of us.

At the age of nineteen I fled the nest. Bye-bye Ruislip, hello Northwood, ten minutes up the road. It felt liberating yet still safe as Mum and Dad were nearby in case I couldn't work out how to pay the gas bill or use the washing machine. I was full of the naive excitement of any young person freeing themselves from the clutches of the parental eye – buzzing with decor ideas and proud of the fridge that only stored milk and vodka. Pure freedom. For me!

Yet for my parents, especially my mum, I imagine it was really quite tricky to see me leave. My truth was that adulthood had hit and I was heading off alone to supermarket sweep Sainsbury's and lie in bed until midday. My mum's truth was that one of her kids had moved on. Her role then had to change. Obviously, she was, is and always will be my mum but what this meant for her on a daily basis changed. There would be no more checking on me at 3 a.m. to make sure I had gotten back from the local nightclub, Destiny, in one piece. There would be no more Linda McCartney sausages cooked for me while I watched *Neighbours* on the couch. She would have more time, more space and probably a lot of questions about how she had spent the last nineteen years of her life – and about what was next.

As much as I am often totally exhausted by my own

children, and usually drowning in laundry and sleep deprivation, I am not looking forward to the day they decide they want to move out or go to uni. I know I will struggle to let go of the maternal role I have so willingly taken on. As our circumstances change, the way our truth manifests itself will change, and our needs will be different so good communication is key. I don't think I knew what good communication was at nineteen. I waltzed out of the family home with a Mini full of trainers and cushions and hoped I would be all right.

As parents, our circumstances change constantly. We must adapt the roles we align ourselves with and the jobs we think make up who we are. This is ever-changing and with those changes come both gain and loss. When I left home, my mum was left to deal with the transition of me leaving and what that meant for her. Less cooking and cleaning for sure, but also perhaps a sense of loss of the role of being an active mother, which had defined her for so long. Although, I could be completely wrong and maybe my mum popped the champs open as soon as I waltzed out the door!

STOP, RECALIBRATE, ALLOW

After scary moments of change, even when we are still full of doubt, new opportunities naturally unfurl. In order to allow in the new, we have to allow space. So often we say we want our lives to be different, but then we hesitate when it comes to making any significant change to the current set-up.

We want a better relationship, but don't leave our current

partner; we want a new job, but can't find the motivation to quit the current one; we want more time to care for ourselves but won't lose any commitments from our busy lives. That last one for me is BIG. I want to be a present, fun, costume-for-World-Book-Day-making mum but I also want to be successful at work, oh, and maybe do some exercise and paint on the side and possibly have a bit of a social life. Then I whine to my husband that I have NO TIME FOR MYSELF! My truth is screaming for change but I won't let it in. I hold up a sign saying, 'I do not have time for this. I'm far too busy and important.'

The Covid-19 pandemic offered up the most startling opportunity for me to look at how much I try to cram into my life and the reasons behind it. In the modern world, we all overcomplicate our lives by thinking we will feel better or perhaps happier if we do more, have more and experience more. I recently heard a phrase I had not been previously acquainted with: 'the optimisation of self'. Oh god, this sounds scary, what is this? I broke it down after hearing it for the first time to see if I could work out why I felt scared of it. My interpretation of its meaning is that we have to get the most out of life and out of ourselves to feel good. A classic modern-day concept that people run with and then focus on way too much rather than what is really going on.

This new phrase made me want to run for the hills because I don't believe it to be true. I am understanding as I mature and gain more life experience that it's not about how much we do, seek or experience; I believe it's about HOW we do all of those things. My life is now about doing things I love and really engaging with that moment, seeking things

I know could be interesting and really learning from them and experiencing things fully. It's not about the quantity of experiences we have in life but much more how we choose to engage with all of the experiences that come our way, good and bad.

During lockdown, though, none of us has been able to strive for the optimisation of self or life. We have had to keep things very bloody simple and, you know what? I have enjoyed that part of it greatly. I haven't enjoyed hearing about the loss, the relentlessness of it all for the NHS workers, or those who feel desperately lonely. BUT I have enjoyed the simplicity. I have previously massively bought into this notion that I have to be doing a lot and experiencing a lot to feel OK. That's what the modern world tells us, so we strive and reach for everything we can get our hands on, then still end up feeling flat. In lockdown, I have felt pure joy in the totally normal. I haven't looked for joy in these moments or striven to find it but it has jumped out at me regardless.

On my daily walk with the kids, looking up at one particular giant, wise old oak with a backdrop of blue sky and BOOM – happiness. Walking barefoot in our garden, which I usually take for granted. It's not a huge or grand garden, but just walking around with the grass beneath my feet has given me a sense of grounding and happiness without reason or explanation. Watching my kids navigate being together twenty-four-seven without the classroom to separate them has taught me a lot and allowed me a sneaky, deeper look into their minds which has been a privilege. JOY!

We assume that toned abs, a new pair of shoes, a weekend crammed with lunches and nights out with mates, big parties, exotic holidays and the most achieved will deliver happiness and joy but I have learned that for me that is never going to be the case. We have all had to slow the hell down (unless of course you work for the NHS or in a care home, are teaching, bus driving (shout-out to Uncle Mick), in a supermarket, etc. – you angel types!) and that has meant discovering joy in new ways. It's also meant we have had to stop trying to find joy and have had to learn to let it appear on its own schedule. What a fun and novel concept. We cannot buy joy, we cannot hunt for it, we cannot tell it to show up, it just arrives when it wants to and usually in the very small, normal and everyday parts of life.

So this has led to me having to ask myself the question, 'WHY THE HELL AM I TRYING TO DO SO MUCH?' Some of it may be to distract from the truth, my truth. Is it because I believe my busyness might bring self-worth or respect from others? At times, maybe it's because I have bought into this whole 'optimisation of self' thing.

I have learned during this lockdown that sometimes you have to surrender even when you really, really don't want to. In fact, that is the meaning of surrender – allowing what is happening instead of resisting it. At the time of writing, bang in the middle of lockdown, I have felt suffocated by my workload. Lucky, I know! I have been able to keep a few of my projects running and adapt others, but they require an insane amount of time and energy all while trying to be super, home-schooling mum and loving wife, oh, and also not losing my cool over the fact that my house looks as messy as my head feels. I have had to surrender and admit that I cannot do it all. My priority is the family and not being a ratty, stressed mum, so that has meant letting go of some work opportunities and also delegating the things I cannot cope with. Delegating is my worst nightmare, because, have I mentioned I'm a massive control freak? There is no normal right now so learning to go with a new pace, a simpler set-up, less work, less social activity and fewer big experiences has been integral and surprisingly wonderful. My new mantra is DO LESS. Maybe it's even my new truth!

None of it has been easy, though. My ego loves to stop change happening even when I know it is needed.

When our wants and needs change – whether that's falling out of love with a person, job, friend, location, path in life or something else – our truth screams for space. We have to allow the process of change to take place by giving it room to breathe:

First we need to STOP.

Then RECALIBRATE – align with what is, rather than what was.

Then ALLOW newness in.

We have to be willing rather than forceful, optimistic instead of demanding. We must surrender rather than push. It's tough as we want results quickly but I've learned that to honour our truth we have to go through this process.

STOP

The first part is really shit-scary! Stopping! AHHH! I hate stopping; it's my number one fear. What will it feel like to be still? How will I cope without my security blanket of busy-ness? What will come up and haunt me?

Stopping means sitting with our thoughts and fears.

It means acknowledging the unknown and accepting the understanding that, despite what we might like to think, we are never really in control (none of us like this one). It means letting go. As I've discussed previously, I'm terrible at letting go, yet often my truth shouts so loudly, especially in the middle of the night when the sky is black velvet and the silence is all-encompassing. I've fought many three-in-the-morning battles with my relentless truth!

This can come to us as what we often refer to as a 'gut' feeling or instinct. We've all experienced this sensation when we feel our truth has changed and we know we need action. The feeling is visceral and big and demands attention. Sometimes we try to mute the sound of it by keeping very busy or driving or eating or shopping. If we can discipline ourselves to properly stop then we have to deal with what lies in front of us.

RECALIBRATE

Once we have noticed our true feelings and what change might mean we can then begin to recalibrate. We start to look at what positive actions might be needed to make that change happen. How you'll live without your partner of six years, how you'll find money if you change job, how you'll create comfort in a new country. This is the part I like more as I get to be pragmatic, which suits me just fine. In my case, Virgoan lists are made and outcomes are estimated. It is a place of action and planning and possibility, excitement and dread too but that's to be expected. It's the moment before the unknown takes hold. Next up you just have to allow it.

ALLOW

This part I find tricky. I have to once again let go and allow the change to take place. I have to surrender to the outcome and hope for the best. If you too find this tricky, look at where that resistance might lie for you. For me, it's all in the fear of fucking up. I don't want to make a mistake and that holds me back from letting go of something I may have outgrown. I don't want to be responsible for messing up my life or someone else's so at times the ALLOWING bit feels very daunting indeed. A healthy dose of trust is necessary – in yourself and in the future.

I recently read *Untamed*, a book by Glennon Doyle, in which she talks in depth about her decision to leave her husband to marry the woman she had fallen in love with. The worry and concern of taking this life-changing step ran deep as she had three children with her husband and a whole life that revolved around her family set-up. Leaving felt terrifying as she wanted her children to be OK, yet she couldn't ignore her truth and what it was now calling her towards. She navigated her children's concerns and fears and her own worries about how it might affect them. Ultimately, she decided to leave her marriage and pursue love with her now wife as she knew that visibly living her own truth was so important to teach her children to honour theirs too. Give that brilliant book a read if you want some great stories about courage and confidence.

POSITIVE CHANGE WITHOUT FEAR

So far in this chapter, we've focused mostly on the negatives of change. I fully acknowledge how scary and damaging change might feel in the moment but let me assure you there are so many juicy pluses too.

What about those moments when our truth leads us to big change and it doesn't feel scary? What about when it feels like our parachute has opened and we are gracefully gliding with a wide-screen gaze over life below us? These are the golden moments when we know we are on the right path. Momentum builds and everything seems to fall into place without much effort. We feel supported and safe and we no longer question the change we have made. It is human instinct to worry about change, or fear that if it was all too easy there must be a hard time coming later, but I think it is so important for us to remember to enjoy these moments so we can have some pockets of freedom and joy.

Can you think of those moments where your truth led you to important and much-needed change and you felt pure freedom? Are there any moments of euphoria that have a cinematic quality to them? Excuse me while I go off on a short self-indulgent romp here but I love recalling mine. I adore selecting these moments from my memory bank so I can remember that this freedom is available to me whenever I need it. I need reminding that I am someone who is capable of letting go and enjoying life without worry and constant panic that something awful is on the horizon.

After my engagement broke off I felt very flat, as the prospect of turning thirty without the partner or kids I had imagined by that age seemed terrifying. God! Looking back, as I now approach forty, I know this was a premature worry but back then it felt like time was whizzing by too quickly. As I mentioned earlier, my dear friend Laura and I decided to book a last-minute trip to Mexico. We both managed to wangle a week off work and, before we knew it, were bleary-eyed, holding giant coffees at the airport at an unfriendly hour. Laura was having a tough time at work doing regular night shifts that finished at 5 a.m. She was jittery with the agitation of someone with two phones and a demanding job. I was flat and a little broken.

During this trip, I gave myself the space with little distraction so I didn't fall back into nostalgia about my old relationship. Without doing much at all, I started to feel differently. I began to realise I would be OK. This shift of focus didn't feel scary or like I was taking a risk – I just felt calm and grounded. With this little new epiphany came a sense of calm that allowed me to make better choices than I had before. My self-worth seemed to grow without my needing it to be attached to another person. My truth was that I would be OK alone.

I clearly remember a moment of total freedom during this trip. A segment of time so free of thought or analysis. A meditation without effort or will. It was 7 p.m. so the sun had lost its fierce burn and was soft, delicate and orange. I had a beer in hand, my body felt loose. Each muscle properly relaxed, maybe for the first time in years. London had left my body. Each busy street, flicking traffic light and screeching car had left my system and my muscles understood this. Laura, my mate and accomplice in mischief in my twenties (and still my dear friend in my thirties), was in the shower after a long day of cycling and swimming. Bedouin Soundclash rippled through the air from the nearby speaker, every note allowing me to slip deeper into the knowledge that I was safe. I was OK. The sky seemed further away than normal, as if it was giving me space and freedom. I stared at the sky without phone in hand, without book under nose, without the distraction of another. I was happy. I was content without attaching that feeling to anything in particular. That joy wasn't about another person, an experience, a compliment, an achievement. It simply WAS. In this moment, I knew I would be OK. My truth had shifted from one of sadness that my engagement had been called off to one of deep knowing that I would thrive again.

I weirdly often get this feeling of everything being fine when I'm on a flight and above the clouds. As soon as the plane bursts through the dense, grey London blanket of cloud and reveals bright, vibrant, life-affirming blue above, I feel OK. I am able to connect with the knowledge that all will be well no matter what is going on back down below on the crowded streets with their sea of phones and cross-wired emails. It seems that gaining physical distance from the chaos below allows me a little more perspective. Recently, I spoke with my mate Gerad Kite, affectionately known as Gezza, and he explained there is actually a five-element acupuncture point called 'above the clouds' which helps reach this exact state.

THE SLOW WINDING ROAD
TO CONFIDENCE

More recently, I have begun to access the same grounded knowingness both in my work and in the relationship I have with myself. After a couple of years of depression swimming around my ankles, then steadily climbing higher and higher towards my heart, I lost my confidence. It just vanished. At work, I felt like a fake and at home I felt like a mess. The darkness swirled and took bites out of me while hissing acerbic comments and flashing up painful memories I wanted to forget. I forgot how to speak – not just my truth but at all. Every word felt disingenuous and at times pointless. I forgot how to enjoy myself or even what I had enjoyed in the past. I had no clue anymore about anything. The inky heaviness made me assume that everyone thought I was awful, stupid, worthless and no fun. I truly believed this and let it take hold of me. My truth was smothered. Blanket-covered, it couldn't breathe or thrive.

I am out the other side of this soul-sucking depression today, which suggests a big change within and a reveal of my truth along the way. Getting through the heaviness was not an overnight moment or a sun-soaked epiphany in Mexico. It was a slow, incremental rebuilding of myself. Brick by brick I built up my confidence over the course of about five years. This is not a tale of complete recovery. There are still days that feel sodden with lifeless depression but the time I referred to happened to be one big block without a break. Endless, without light. I'm most definitely out of that.

Some days I would kick down what I had painstakingly

217

remade and end up falling way back into the bad thought patterns. On other days, I would let experience and good people help me build new parts of me – friends sharing their own pain and experience, having ideas for new projects and my children's grounding and love. The bricks slowly rose and I started to get the fire in my belly again.

At some point, I guess the confidence and willingness to let go becomes bigger, and therefore more powerful, than the depression and you start to feel, well . . . like yourself. The truth slowly makes its ways to the surface. I began to recognise that I was not an awful person who everyone hates. I started to understand that I was good at my job, creating new relationships and giving things a go. I reconnected with the knowledge that I enjoyed painting, reading, being in nature, cooking delicious food, laughing with mates. The truth rose to the top like small bursting bubbles releasing me each time.

This shift and realisation of my truth was slow and at times very stop-start but it felt like a good change nonetheless. A change of heart and a change eventually of mind. My truth changed for the better and it didn't feel scary at all – it was just hard work at times. In these instances, I think support is needed to help the change along. You need good people in your life who can support the rebuilding of YOU and who understand it won't happen overnight. People who are in it with you for the long haul. Those friends you know will cast a line out to sea to drag you back to shore even if it's 3 a.m. The kind of friends who won't judge you or allow you to sink further in murkiness. The kind you know you can bare your soul to, warts and all. You don't need hundreds of mates, just one or two really quality mates who GET YOU. If you feel you are lacking this in life or that your friends don't understand your experience, speaking to a professional is a good idea. That could be your local GP, or a charity like Mind or the Samaritans.

This sort of change isn't an epiphany or quick fix, it's the long winding road to knowing who you are and what you are about. It's a less sexy story than the flash of inspiration, as we all want something fast and efficient, but it's more sustainable and it lasts longer.

We want our truth to be revealed immediately, we want the pain of change to be over and done with, we have zero patience. The faster, slicker, modern world with its 5G, same-day delivery, fast-food story tells us waiting is bad and slow is for losers. But what if taking the long, slow route is better? What if that means long-lasting results and a better understanding?

From experience, I think this sort of incremental change is very valuable. Although feeling scared is good, as we learn to challenge ourselves, I don't believe that every good change has to be scary. I don't believe all gut decisions are made in one moment and play out in the next. I think sometimes when our truth changes it is wonderful for it to be slow, thoughtful, measured and without pain. We can change as quickly or slowly as we desire. There is no race. No one is judging us from above and no one will mark us at the end of our journeys with a big fat ten on a score card (or a zero). We have the right to be as cautious and thoughtful as we feel is right and those around us have to try to understand that. Although often with our own truth there is little choice as we know deep down what the answers are, the pace is a choice. The speed set and time travelled are up to you.

Recently I spoke with Alicia Keys on my Happy Place podcast, who talked about those moments where there is a decision to be made and you have a 'resounding YES'. It might be an instant feeling of what is correct for you, so then you have to be wary of the rumination that follows, when you might talk yourself out of something great. I quizzed Alicia as to whether she believed a 'maybe' should therefore always be a 'no'. She said that a maybe could slowly turn into a resounding yes with a little research and self-education on a matter. That gave me so much clarity on how I might go about making decisions in the future. There will be moments where decisions feel instant and easy to make, but there will also be slow maybes that grow into beautiful resounding yeses!

Maybe you'll go off on wonderful tangents and discover new things about yourself. God, I didn't think I'd be writing books for a living when I was in my twenties! I thought unless I was on TV forever I would be a failure but one delicious tangent has been writing about life and learning so much from doing so. It's now my favourite thing I do. Sometimes we think we know ourselves so well, but by allowing a little digression and curiosity we can really start to reveal the truth. It might stay the same shape for years, it might swell and reduce, it might hide and reappear and it might change altogether. There is no wrong or right as long as you are listening to it.

NAN

As I've been mulling over this chapter I've thought back to the many times I've left relationships because I felt differently about the partner, departed workplaces because my needs changed and fell out of friendships due to my views changing. But what if my truth hasn't changed at all? Bear with me. Maybe incrementally as we age and grow we just get more in touch with it. Maybe life is one big board game where we get nearer and nearer to our own truth. Layers are peeled back to reveal what was there all along. Could that be it? Could it be less about change and more of a reveal? I can sense that in myself to a degree for sure.

Remember how we talked about our inner child at the start of the book? How we are born with truth shining out of our hearts? Well, maybe this process of finding our truth is less of a discovery of something new and more of a regression back to the simple truth that has always been within us. It might manifest in different ways as we grow and age, but the truth remains the foundation.

Think about all the home truths your grandparents may have dished out to you or those around you over the years. My nan Ruby would come out with comical things about me or others in her vicinity and, even after watching them physically wince, she would sit there feeling confident in her conviction. With her purple hair coiffed and curled, she would proudly sit with her peach-painted nails in her lap quite literally saying what she saw. Once I visited her in her care home and was greeted with, 'OH, look at your PINK hair, oh *Fearne*,' followed by a slight tut. Please note her aforementioned PURPLE HAIR! Genius. Ruby was a wonderful force of Welsh nature and would never hold back. Yet she was at peace with it. She didn't beat herself up mentally after saying something aloud or spend hours at night worrying about it. It was all said with good intent even if it didn't come out that way; Ruby knew that the reaction to her stark truth-telling was purely down to the receiver of the comment. There's something in that for sure.

As we age, we seem to get more and more honest. More and more in touch with who we really are and what we are about. More and more confident in what we want to say and how we want to say it. It seems like a very general, sweeping statement to make, as some are in touch with their honesty all along. But the magnetic people in life who inspire us and lead the way are the minority – for most of us, it's a gradual climb and an incremental reveal of our truth over a lifetime. Isn't that quite exciting? I take a lot of comfort from the thought that all of us are constantly moving ever closer to who we really are and what we are about.

How has your truth changed
over the years?

_____

_____

_____

_____

_____

_____

_____

What might your truth look like in the
future if you let go of all inhibition and
concern about what others think?

_____

_____

_____

_____

_____

_____

_____

_____

10

TRUTH TELLERS

When we are feeling a little uncertain or shaky in our own truth, it can be very handy to remind ourselves of those who speak theirs without apology. Those who are clear, confident and care little about what people around them or the outside world think. They can offer example and inspiration to help us unearth our own truth and how we might choose to speak it.

We may assume that those who are already speaking their truth are successful, shiny, with big personalities and big lives, yet this is not always the case. You may have watched me on TV, seen me on Instagram or read my books and assumed I had it all sorted and confidently speak my truth all the time. If that was the case, I doubt I would have ended up with a sizeable cyst clogging up my throat and I certainly wouldn't have bothered writing this book! In fact, writing this book has been the perfect place to remind myself of my own truth. I've dissected it and turned it over in my palm. I've squirmed and felt my toes curling in my socks when looking at the moments where I have ignored my truth altogether, and I hope that by sharing this with you it may help you do the same. It's been an honour to spend time really reacquainting myself with some of my inner truths. I think not speaking up has been one of my greatest challenges as an adult. I've been stifled by not knowing how to open my mouth and say what I feel and I've been bullied, overpowered, manipulated and drowned out by others because of this. I'm sure many of you feel the same, so who can inspire us to be bolder in our truth?

I know a ton of people in the public eye or in positions of power who appear secure in who they are and would respond robustly if another was to challenge them but, in real life, under the layers of TV make-up, titles given, awards showered, money thrown, things bought, they feel like everybody else. Unsure. Unsure of themselves and their truth. Actually, sometimes I think many people who are seemingly successful actually attach too much of their self-worth to their achievements and how widely they are accepted and liked rather than how they feel about themselves outside of that. I know this because when I'm not following my truth and feeling good inside I will allow outside applause to affect how I feel about myself. I cling onto it hoping it might top me back up. All it does, of course, is delay you in sorting your shit out properly.

ASSUMPTIONS AND PAPS

Remember that most of what we think about others is assumption only. Most is based on what we see on the outside, which counts for very little indeed. The person with the beautiful big house and pristine car might feel trapped and as though they have little purpose, therefore ignoring their truth altogether. The Instagram account you follow that gives the impression of an adventurous and problem-free life might be an effort to project an alternative life to the one being led on the other side of the camera. The ambitious working mum you see at the school gates who seems to have it all down and manages to get a weekly blow-dry might be struggling inside with keeping her shit together and her truth might be screaming for a simpler set-up. We just don't know.

It is imperative we don't make assumptions about those who seem to be living and speaking their truth and we mustn't confuse surface or material success for happiness, contentment or a life driven from a place of truth. Towards the end of my tenure at Radio 1, a DJ from BBC London told me she would look out of the window at me being papped every day thinking I had it all. I seemed to have the attention and busyness around me that we all assume in the modern world means success. I explained that, most mornings, I struggled with this bombardment of attention. I would feel excruciatingly embarrassed that lovely people in the local coffee shop going about their day had to endure this ridiculous circus and might make assumptions about me that weren't true – that I was somehow courting the publicity or had set it up to happen. During some of that time I was struggling mentally and I sometimes felt hollow inside, so I really didn't fancy having a camera shoved in my face before 8 a.m. For all my outward appearance of success, I wasn't living my truth back then, and I certainly didn't feel I was able to speak it. I knew I needed change and perhaps some time out to make sense of the madness that I had gotten so used to.

My truth is that I prefer being in my home in comfy clothes (preferably with no bra on), drinking tea and reading books to being papped on the way to work. My truth is that I sometimes find the pressure of live radio too much to bear and prefer writing, where I know I can take my time, edit and form sentences with thought and clarity. My truth is that I often prefer to be unseen in the shadows rather than in the spotlight with all eyes judging and commenting.

Even though, at one time, change felt too big and scary, incrementally I've been able to move into a space where I can live my truth pretty much daily. The lovely BBC London presenter who assumed I was revelling in the attention and flashing bulbs hadn't been able to see that beneath the outward drama and morning ceremony there was someone who didn't feel she was living her truth at all.

LOUD DOESN'T MEAN CONFIDENT

Also, we must not mistake outward brash confidence for inner knowing. I've met so many people who are loud, opinionated and don't mind butting in. I have felt small when around them and have retreated inside, becoming a mute shrew who patiently waits to be spoken to. I'm not good around people like this as I get too in my own head. The balance tips too much and I willingly take on the role of the quiet one.

I think a lot of people who appear outwardly confident are actually covering up something else entirely. Not always, but sometimes. Those who appear highly opinionated might not be running purely on truth. Maybe they're channelling fear from something very personal? Maybe they have deep, unaddressed sorrow or anger, so being opinionated and shouting others down gives them a way to vent? Perhaps they feel lacking in some way so any attention, in any form, fills a void.

If they've caught me on a good day, some people might have at times assumed I'm overly confident, loud and opinionated. I have been known to talk a lot but mainly either because I'm insanely excited about something and I want to talk it into reality, or I'm insanely nervous so let my jittery-energy party-popper words out of my mouth at an alarming rate. But when I'm dealing with stuff, I go inwards. I go quiet and slow and I can't communicate well at all. If someone says to me, 'Can I have a word?' and beckons to a quiet corner I SHIT MYSELF. I don't feel I can hold my own in that space. What do they want to talk about? I instantly feel like I'm at school about to get bollocked. I forget I'm a grown adult who is allowed to defend herself, have her say and disagree. Note to self: must remember this next time.

EAT, PRAY, LOVE

Let's look at the other side of the coin. Those who are very quiet around others might be deemed shy or, conversely, massively confident because they don't feel the need to show themselves. Sometimes they can even be perceived as rude. We can all make assumptions based on how someone acts but I think when you meet someone who is living their truth, you FEEL it.

When I meet someone who is living their truth I KNOW! I can smell it, sense it and am left obsessing about them for days afterwards. I am a person easily intoxicated by the strength and charisma of another. Their energy lingers and gives me fire in my belly. It extracts my own truth as I know it is OK and safe to be who I am. If they can, I can. They can lead the way, I'll follow. To meet someone who walks around knowing what they stand for and how they need to interact with others is a delicious feeling. You know exactly where you stand with people who embody the truth and you feel inspired to do the same.

I've long been a huge fan of Elizabeth Gilbert, having read *Eat Pray Love* not long after it was published in 2006. The book is based on Elizabeth's need to live her truth. She left a marriage and travelled the world, but this wasn't her acting on a whim – it was her moving with her truth and need for self-exploration. That book changed me and solidified my understanding of the importance of one's truth. I didn't necessarily understand this at the time but I sensed I needed to tune in to something deeper more often. The book is about risk-taking and not worrying what others think – again something I needed to focus on after years of being told openly and constantly what others think of me.

In 2019, I found myself in a 'pinch me now' moment. Somehow, during Elizabeth's book tour for her novel *City of Girls* she ended up on my Happy Place podcast. We had not met before yet the warmth and calm I had imagined from her was instantly present. Slightly nervous on our first meeting, I gabbled away in an overly apologetic tone about how I had a copy of my own book, *Happy*, for her, which was potentially cringe but would she take one anyway. She graciously popped it in her bag.

I only calmed down once we entered the studio, which indeed is my very own 'happy place'. I feel in control with podcast mic in hand. I'm not about to wing it or venture off into unknown territory without knowing how to get back on track. I work for weeks in advance of each episode to research the person I'm chatting to and think about other interesting life subjects we might riff around. Elizabeth felt open. Her heart, her spirit, her mind were open. For many, this is a vulnerable place to be but when you are living your truth you can answer any question and talk about any subject brought up because you are confident in your story and your beliefs. When you are secure in your truth, you can't really be challenged or go wrong in conversation because you will always have an appropriate answer. It might not always be agreeable to all others, but of course if you're living your truth you don't care.

Elizabeth and I weaved and waltzed around so many subjects and I found myself relaxing even more. I found my heart opening up and my mind calming. My truth was starting to show up for me too. Her confidence was contagious. Elizabeth is the epitome of living in truth. Even if she is talking about tough times or moments of perceived mistake she comes from a place of truth so the words formed feel strong and robust and unapologetic.

I had a thing or two to learn here. I've often been so apologetic in interviews and in general conversation. Apologising for my success in case it makes people feel uncomfortable, for my failures in case I'm judged; apologising for my opinion in case it offends anyone; apologising for my *lack* of opinion in case I offend anyone; apologising for being too much, too little, too loud, too quiet. I've apologised my way out of so many situations as I assume I will then come away unscathed. I will be untouched by opinion or judgement and can then sleep that night. But the cyst! The lump of swallowed words is the physical sign that repression of my true self isn't the best way. I would sleep much better at night if I learned to stop apologising for who I am and just got on with letting the world hear me roar. So what if others don't like how loud it might come out? How can opinion hurt me if I know MY truth?

Here was Elizabeth sat in front of me, showing me exactly how it's done. A master in truth, a maven of personal knowing, a slayer of all self-doubt. You cannot walk away from a chat like that feeling the same. I would be foolish to sleepwalk away thinking my life could carry on as it was before. When you've experienced the real deal, you cannot ignore what you've witnessed. I'm not saying that I walked out of the studio and then started living and speaking my truth instantly but that conversation is a place I return to regularly as I know that my own truth is in there waiting to emerge with as much strength and tenacity as Elizabeth's. I now follow her on Instagram to get a top-up or read one of her many brilliant books when I need refuelling. These experiences feel heady in the moment but, like perfume, fade over time so it's important to keep remembering and revisiting. Not just recalling the words spoken but the feeling that the individual had around them.

SPEAKING YOUR TRUTH DOESN'T MEAN YOU HAVE TO ROAR

Individuals with an air of calm and collectedness seem rare today. It's a fact that most of us feel stressed, anxious and sleep and eat badly and this epidemic of anxiety is down to the fact that we are not living our truth as a society. We are constantly seeking comfort in outside sources. We believe the lies we are told that more means better and that we must keep striving to have it all. This of course leaves us feeling empty, so we try to fill that hole. We stuff food into it hoping it'll go away, we watch TV for hours numbing our fears and worries. We shun sleep in favour of drinking too much or working until our eyes sting from looking at a laptop. I'm pretty sure our truth isn't found in any of those places.

For most of us, I believe our truth can be found by being in nature more, resting more, eating better, talking to friends more, working less, sleeping more, looking at the sky more, thinking less and doing less. But the modern world tells us the opposite. The modern world tells us our worth depends on doing more, achieving more, sleeping less, eating less, showing off more, keeping busy and aiming for success.

Going back to Elizabeth (I know, I know, I'll move on in a minute but I'm obsessed!), she does all the things that align to her truth. If you follow her on social media you'll see she places importance on the simple things but talks about the small bits of life in BIG ways. She honours friendship, a good sunset, buying stationery as it makes her feel good, reading lovely books, eating, resting under trees. You might have judgement around certain people living their truth and think, 'Well, it's all right for them, they've got the time and money to sit under trees reading.' But why is Elizabeth or anyone else living life to their own beat any different to us? Yes, she is fortunate to have her health which allows her some physical freedom, but actually a lot of her contentment is due to making changes. Elizabeth left a good job, her husband and her home to follow her gut with no back-up plan before writing *Eat Pray Love*. More recently, she cared for her dying partner and dealt with the grief that followed, but she still kept following her truth. She is still doing that today.

We all have the power to speak up – to those around us and to the world. We can communicate with our voices, a pen, laptop or via social media in any way we desire. It is our choice to feel the freedom of speaking our truth fully to others. Speaking your truth is not a privilege some have and some don't. There will always be risk involved no matter what your story is.

Look at Malala Yousafzai. She was shot in the head to keep her quiet. She was a schoolgirl with no platform at all. No audience or group who would listen. But she stood up and she spoke about girls' right to education. She bellowed her truth to all who would hear and put her life on the line to do so. She was not someone who had privilege or security, but her heart sang loudly to her to jump into the unknown.

She has been able to create astonishing change for young women all around the world. She has given others a voice and the power to know they deserve to learn and be taught. She has calmly used words to elevate the needs of other young women and to drown out the cries from those who resort to violence. Speaking your truth and creating change doesn't have to mean you roar.

LOOK TO BE INSPIRED

Some may have power, a platform and a lot of people listening but if they're not speaking their truth then what is the point? I can't imagine it feels good to stand up in front of a lot of people and lie. I can't imagine that feels fulfilling afterwards or allows a deep and decent night's sleep with a clear conscience. Being untruthful from a position of great influence may get the desired results and allow someone to hold onto power but it can't feel great.

Some aim for power rather than responsibility and that is a huge shame. I always view power as such a vapid and ephemeral notion. It's something that those who feel lacking in themselves cling onto with white knuckles. Responsibility seems much more appealing – a space where you know you can help with genuine change and make a difference. I would much rather have a smaller crowd, an engaged crowd, or one friend who knows I am being real. That is a proper transaction and a meaningful connection forged in truth.

It can seem terrifying that we have world leaders and

politicians who don't use their position to speak their truth, or the truth at all, so we have to focus on those we know who do. It is up to us to seek out those in a place of power, or those who aren't powerful but speak with integrity, who are deeply connecting with what is real. Luckily, we have good examples of that in the modern world. We can pick up incredible books where people have poured out their personal story and given us their hearts. Bryony Gordon has a collection of insanely honest books that inspire truth-telling. Poorna Bell writes with a poetic flair that summons her truth to the top. Gabrielle Bernstein helps change other people's lives in her inspiring books by pouring out her truth onto the page. Jedidiah Jenkins's *To Shake the Sleeping Self* ignited a confidence in truth-telling for me as I inhaled large chunks of this book before bed.

We can watch films where others have painted beautiful true stories on the screen for us to be inspired by. I love *Wild*, which stars Reese Witherspoon and is based on a book written by Cheryl Strayed. *Milk*, which is set in the 1970s, depicts the courage of gay politician Harvey Milk who campaigned for LGBTQ+ rights in San Francisco. And – obviously! – *Eat Pray Love*, not only written by Elizabeth Gilbert but starring Julia Roberts.

We have activists who put themselves on the line for judgement and struggle every day. Greta Thunberg who relentlessly travels the world by boat staging school strikes for climate change while being constantly shouted down by grown men; Tarana Burke who kicked off the #MeToo movement, giving so many people a voice who had previously felt too scared or ashamed to come forward to talk about their own experience of sexual abuse. I'm 100 per cent sure that standing up to say their bit wasn't relaxing and required – and still requires – a huge dose of courage and strength, yet they must soldier on and they must keep speaking their truth.

There are so many artists and bands that have the ability to make me weak at my knees as their words feel like my story and their feelings spark my truth. Where do I start? There is a Fleet Foxes song that I adore called 'Naiads Cassadies', which is all about looking at who stole your light and started your own self-loathing. At one particular time, that was my truth so the song made me sit up and think about who I had allowed to steal my light and make me self-loathe. The power of one line in a song! I love Hozier as his lyrics are bursting with an inquisitive question mark over love and life. The song 'Movement' from his last album is sublime and makes me feel ever more in love with words and how you can play with them. We listen to a lot of old soul music in the house as well and I think the artists of that genre really sang their truth out. Nina Simone lets her pain rip out of her with every bold tone. Music can connect you to your truth and allow emotions to flow freely.

Outside of popular culture and activism, we also all have friends who are willing to go there for themselves and for us, unearthing their own truth whenever it is needed. We have doctors and nurses who follow their truth and carry out daily service to enable others to carry on living their truth. We have painters depicting otherworldly scenes that capture our imagination and unlock our truth. We have teachers and mentors speaking their truth to inspire others.

We have David Attenborough trying to wake us all the hell up to look at our planet, which is what gets forgotten due to consumerism and speed. We have carers who use their truth to care and nurture. And we have ourselves.

When you feel it is hard to connect to your truth, remember there is inspiration out there from others.

SPEAKING MY TRUTH

As I neared the end of writing this book, my voice started to clear. I was much less Rod Stewart and much more Mariella Frostrup after a hot lemon and honey. I started recording podcasts again and kind of forgot that I was booked in to have a throat operation in a week's time. I went back into the hospital for a pre-op scan to check in on Mr Cyst. The tiny camera snaked down towards the back of my throat, once again making my toes curl inside my shoes in discomfort. My nasal cavity came into view, then the back of my throat and then the fleshy gates of truth. My vocal cords. My glistening, pink, quivering and CYST-FREE vocal cords. The doctor laughed as I stared at the screen with wide eyes. My husband was going to be gutted! He was so looking forward to my two weeks of no speaking so he could take control of the house without me interfering with worries about packed lunches made with the incorrect fruit-to-sandwich ratio.

Now, I'm not saying I miraculously cured myself but could I have helped the process a little by interrogating my ideas around speaking my truth? Apparently, 5 per cent of people who get cysts on their vocal cords find that they naturally disperse and disappear, yet perhaps my change of course personally may have helped the situation a teeny bit?

Whether my writing process managed to help clear this little critter from my throat or not, this cyst incident massively inspired me to keep speaking my truth. Without this little nod from the universe I most likely would not have given this subject matter another thought. I would have continued to create boundary-less work and friendship dynamics; I would have carried on looking for ways to blame others for my own resistance to seeing the truth; I would have stayed small and quiet when I really needed to roar. This situation might not have completely opened me up to my truth all of the time but it has been the most wonderful fast track to strengthening my relationship with honesty, authenticity and integrity.

I now – hopefully with some of you lovely lot – want to continue challenging myself to 'fess up, speak up, dish up whenever I can. I will endeavour to keep focusing more on my truth than other people's lies, to honour what I believe while not being shaken by what I don't and to speak up when the world says NO. I am never going to stop trying to speak my truth.

TEN INSPIRING TRUTH TELLERS

★ **My kids.** At times too honest but it is needed.

★ **My husband.** My truth-telling inspiration always.

★ **David Bowie.** He challenged people in ways they hadn't been challenged before and got them to look at their own truth and view of the world.

★ **Bryony Gordon,** for there is no one more honest on planet earth.

★ **Russell Brand.** Not only a mega brain and acutely skilled at unpicking the truth but also wonderful for honest advice via voice note on a regular basis.

★ **Brené Brown.** Truth with stats! Nothing better.

★ **Lizzo,** who has helped millions of women to celebrate their bodies.

★ **Matt Haig,** who has lifted a lot of weight from many who have felt there is no hope.

★ **Jada Pinkett Smith.** Her *Red Table Talk* Facebook show has taught me a lot and helped me chill the hell out after a long day of parenting.

★ **My mates,** who have always been able to create a balance of total honesty without causing offence over the years. Without them I am lost.

My truth tellers are:

_____

_____

_____

_____

_____

_____

_____

_____

_____

_____

_____

_____

_____

_____

_____

_____

_____

_____

_____

_____

_____

_____

_____

THANK YOUS

Like most things in life, writing a book takes a village so I have a lot of thank-yous to get through. Thank you so much, Orion, for giving me the time and space to write another book. I'm so grateful for the freedom and encouragement received throughout. I find writing so liberating but of course with that comes a little fear, as spilling out your innermost thoughts can feel like standing in your local supermarket with nothing but your pants on (oh, and maybe a mask), so to have Pippa, Rosie, Zoe, Ru, Katie, Jess, Paul, Leanne and Jennifer along for the ride ensured a level of comfort and support that pushed me in the right direction. Thank you so much to all at Orion for ploughing on as normal throughout the pandemic, keeping me on track with deadlines and working so swiftly on the edits. It's once again been a total pleasure.

Thank you, Rabab at Orion, for creating such a beautiful cover. I desperately wanted the cover of this book to look like freedom and you've totally nailed it. Get me to those rosebud-coloured mountains now!

A massive thank you to my literary agent and friend Amanda Harris, who not only believed in this book and cheered me on but was also on hand for many SOS-global-pandemic-help-I-have-kids-and-can't-think-straight chats on text. As a working mum of three, Amanda inspired me through every bleary-eyed writing session and every torturous home-schooling attempt. Amanda, you are amazing.

Holly Bott, Mary Bekhait and Sarah White at YMU Group, I have thanked you all before and will continue to do so in every book I write as you continuously lay the foundations for me to keep creating and working up ideas that I'm passionate about. Without your skill and tenacity I would be a sweating, disorganised mess. You three know only too well that my self-esteem can take a nosedive at any moment, yet you are always there to encourage me to keep on trucking. Thanks for not giving up on me even though I've emailed telling you I'm giving up a million times (did I mention I wrote this book during a pandemic?).

Thanks so much to my husband Jesse, who on many occasions wrestled the kids off me so I could sneak into my quiet corner of the house to get this book out of me. The words were inside all along and I knew I could write it quickly because I felt so passionately about this subject matter, but I needed a little space. Thank you, Jesse, for giving me that time and space to be creative. Yes, we may have aged fifty years in four months due to schools being shut and a lack of activities for kids in 2020, but our partnership is built on the understanding that we both love to create and need space to do so and I think we make a bloody good team.

Thanks to my kids for being amazing under the circumstances. I think most parents feel amazed at how the younger generations have adapted throughout all of this weirdness, potentially much better than we have. Thank you, Rex, Honey, Arthur and Lola, for showcasing such dynamism throughout. Arthur, we are so proud of how you dealt with not being able to sit your A-levels and are so excited for your next adventure at university. All four children (OK Arthur, I know you're now eighteen so a man, but I'm somewhat in denial) teach me how to speak my truth with more courage and vivacity each day. I watch how you stand your ground, communicate with honesty and often without even flinching. I have a lot to learn from you still. I love you with all of my heart.

Thanks to my ma, pa and brother Jamie for always supplying solid grounding, laughter, wisdom and Aperol on tap if needed. Mum and Dad, I have loved seeing your pieces of artwork created during your Friday afternoon art sessions at home during the pandemic. Watching you create each week with dedication certainly kept me on track with my own creativity.

A huge thanks to my dear friends, who I feel so comfortable speaking to in the most truthful way. The conversations I've had with my core group of mates over the years have alleviated pain, given clarity, made me howl with laughter, sent me whirling with nostalgia, boosted my confidence and helped me follow my gut. Even during this strange time with a lack of face-to-face contact we have continued much-needed conversation with WhatsApp voice notes, FaceTime and even the occasional postcard sent ten minutes down the road. God, I love my mates.

My last thank-you is to YOU. I really hope this book has left you feeling that you bloody well deserve to speak your truth. Please know that this is something I'm desperately still working on personally as I think it's something we have to keep practising for the entirety of our lives. There'll be moments where we are all nailing it and other times when we are not, but please know I'm there with you, learning and trying again each time. We've got this!

If you enjoyed this book, you may be interested in Fearne Cotton's previously published bestsellers

Available now in paperback, ebook and audio